# THE INQUIRER'S BIBLE

An understandable version of
the world's greatest love story.

EDITED BY

STEPHEN P SOUZA

**Editor's Note**

This Inquirers' Bible is an abridged re-translation of the Holy Scriptures. It is not intended to be a substitute for the complete Bible, but rather, an introduction for adult readers. Those who are already familiar with the Bible will also find it to be extremely helpful in understanding salvation history. In most Bible studies the student must flip back and forth from book to book and verse to verse and back again in order to understand a particular idea. In this Inquirer's Bible that is already done for you. All you have to do is start at the beginning and read.

No single or particular translation of the Bible was used in compiling this abridged version. Rather, ideas and situations are communicated in free prose. The Bible scholar, when reading this version, will recognize that the flow of the words follows closely the original; however, any match of exact wording to any existing Bible translation is an unintended coincidence.

ISBN: 9798629621959 (paperback)

# Acknowledgements

This publication of The Inquirer's Bible would not be possible without the assistance and contributions of Pamela Souza, Tony Souza, Dr. Keith McAfee, Marcia Cecil, and Laura Keber.

# Introduction

There are men's Bibles, women's Bibles, children's Bibles, Catholic Bibles, Protestant Bibles, commentary Bibles, meditation Bibles, and prayer Bibles; but, until now, there has not really been a Bible that flows. One that the average person can just pick up, read, and understand. That's who this Inquirer's Bible is for; someone who just wants to know the message without getting lost in the process.

Have you ever read the entire Bible? If you said no, you are in the vast majority. Why is it that the most popular, most published, and most read book in human history is a mystery to so many of us? Is it because the Bible is a daunting book? With nearly 800,000 words it is a massive read; and many people find those words to be monotonous at times and confusing at other times. Some find it contradictory and disjointed at times. Few people, including few Christians, have ever read the Bible from beginning to end because it is indeed hard to read. But why is it so hard to read?

The word 'bible' means 'book,' but the Bible is not actually a book. It is a collection of many writings, of widely varying size, style, and purpose, that were written by many people to many different people over a period of around a thousand years. These authors had no idea that, someday, their writings would be compiled into a massive volume, so they did not write with that in mind. Those many writings were read separately and individually for centuries. It was not until over three hundred years after the death and resurrection of Jesus, that Pope Damasus I decreed that, out of the hundreds of old writings that were being read by Christians throughout the world, the seventy-three most reliable of them should be assembled and bound together and should be considered the word of God; a reliable guide for the instruction of all Christians. Thus, was born the Bible as we know it. But very few people knew it because book production was very, very expensive. It was not until eleven centuries later, with the advent of the printing press, that it became economical to include all seventy-three writings within one cover. But it was still a hard read; monotonous, confusing, and disjointed. Yet it endures. There must be something great in it.

The Bible is like a vast quilt; made of many different parts stitched together into a whole. Because there is so much to it, most Christians concentrate on a few of those parts; picking favorite verses to study, and even memorize, without really stepping back to observe the glorious whole that is the sum of the parts. In fact, most people don't realize that the Bible reads like an epic novel; with a setting, conflict, rising action, a climax, falling action, a resolution, and an epilogue. The Bible is a classic romance with a knightly jilted lover, (God), his naive but desirable damsel in distress, (humanity), and an evil prince (Satan), who through deceit, and worse, does his best to entrap the damsel for himself, repeatedly enticing her away from our hero despite his constant faithfulness. It's a long hard struggle filled with tension, misunderstandings, and lost opportunities but, in the end, the hero saves the damsel and they live happily ever after.

This Inquirer's Bible presents the Bible as that epic novel; tracing the thread that binds the different parts together to form a marvelous whole. Nothing of significance was added but several sections not essential to the plot were omitted. You can explore those wonderful writings at the proper time, which is after you have grounded yourself in the story they celebrate. Also omitted is the chapter and verse organizational method that was added centuries after the writings were penned, and which breaks up the flow of the message.

The traditional Bible is divided into two main parts; the Old Testament, which occurred before Jesus, and the New Testament, which occurred after Jesus. This Inquirer's Bible breaks the story into three parts; The Father, the story of the foundational relationship between God and mankind; The Son, the biography of Jesus, which contains the climax of the story; and The Holy Spirit, events, letters, and commentaries that serve as a lengthy epilogue, connecting the message to the reader. The first two books are third person narrations of events in chronological order, from the creation of the world, to the resurrection of Christ. The third book communicates the commentaries of the earliest Christian writers through a series of dialogues that take place between John, the last of the Apostles, and Laurentius, the governor of Patmos, the island to where John was exiled, and where he wrote the last book of the Bible. It is topical and its structure mirrors The Apostles' Creed which is a still popular capsule of Christian thought that pre-dates the Bible. The dialogues are hypothetical, but John's words are Biblical. Though not mentioned in the Bible, the people, places, and events in Book Three were borrowed from Church history to provide a framework for the dialogues, and to personalize the teachings therein for the reader.

Each book is divided into chapters and sections. Each chapter is preceded by a reading from the Book of Psalms, which is a beautiful compilation of Jewish hymns that celebrate and compliment the story. The beginning of each section names the books of the Bible that were referenced in it.

To make this book as easy to read as possible, the archaic language that we associate with the Bible is removed and plain, modern English is used. Also, names are explained because names mean things. When many of the names are mentioned, the meaning of the name is given. For example, Peter means Rock. It was not a name at that time, but was a title Jesus gave to the man. So instead of "Peter," "The Rock" is used since "Rock" is what people of the time would have thought of when they said "Peter." "Church" is substituted with "Assembly" because that is the word that was originally used. On the other hand, "Jesus" is the Greek form of the Jewish name "Joshua" which means "God saves." But, Jesus (Joshua) was a common name at that time so Jesus is called Jesus in this Bible version.

In order to tie events together, or to present them in context, some explanation is woven into the narration from time to time. These explanations are minimal and are consistent with the longest standing and most widely accepted Christian traditions. In the third book, John's words are from scripture while Laurentius provides the historical context.

This is not historic fiction or some kind of free re-telling with artistic license. It is true to the original, but easier to read. Read it like a story, not a textbook. You can dissect it or proof text it later as you like, but if you do, you may miss the greatest story ever told. So, get comfortable, relax, and discover.

# A Message to the Inquirer

*Fear not; the one who has become your husband is your maker; his name is Lord of All. He is your redeemer, called God of all the Earth. You are like a wife abandoned and grieved in spirit; a young wife, married and rejected.*

*Your God says, "For a short time, I abandoned you, but with great tenderness I will take you back. In anger, for a moment, I hid my face from you; but with unending love, I have compassion for you. Just as in the days of Noah, when I swore that the waters shall never again deluge the Earth; so, I have sworn not to be angry with you or to rebuke you. Though the mountains may fall, and the hills may shake, my love for you shall not fail, nor my covenant of peace be shaken.*

*"I will establish you in righteousness and justice, far from fear or oppression, where you will be safe."*

*From the writings of the prophet Isaiah*

# Book I, The Father

1   In His Own Image     3
*God, a Man, and His Wife*

2   You and Your Family, I Will Spare     9
*God, a Man, and His Family*

3   Through You, All the World Shall Be Blessed     12
*God, a Man, and His Clan*

4   This is My Name Forever     33
*God, a Man, and His Nation*

5   God Has Given This Land to You     54
*The Nation Takes Root*

6   There, Said the Lord, Anoint That One     63
*God, A Man, and His Kingdom*

7   Wickedness Burns Like Fire     76
*The Kingdom Ends*

# Book II, The Son
## *God, a Man, and the World*

1   And You Will Name Him Jesus                                    91
    *The Beginning*

2   He Will Increase                                               102
    *The First Year*

3   Follow Me                                                      110
    *The Second Year*

4   You Are the Messiah, the Son of the Living God                 127
    *Third Year*

5   Love One Another as I Have Loved You                           147
    *The Last Week*

6   It is Finished                                                 158
    *The Agony of the Messiah*

7   I Have Seen the Lord                                           167
    *The New Beginning*

# Book lll, The Holy Spirit

1    Do You Understand What You Are Reading?     175
*Memories*

2    The Visible of the Invisible God     184
*On God*

3    The Pillar and Foundation of Truth     190
*On the Church*

4    Be Forgiving, and You Will Be Forgiven     195
*On the Forgiveness of Sins*

5    Faith, Hope, and Love     201
*On the Christian Life*

6    Give All Your Cares to Him, For He Cares For You     206
*On Prayer*

7    I Make All Things New     211
*The Letter*

# BOOK I
## THE FATHER


## Covenant

A usually formal, solemn, and binding agreement: Merriam Webster

# 1

# In His Own Image

## God, a Man, and His Wife

*When I see your heavens, the work of your hands, the moon and the stars-what are mortal men that you care for them? Yet you have made them little less than divine and crowned them with honor and glory. You have given them rule over your creation, put all things at their feet; sheep and oxen, even wild animals, and the birds of the air, and the fish of the sea. Oh Lord, our God, how great is your name!*

*Psalm 8*

## In the Beginning
From the Book of Genesis

In the beginning, when God created the heavens and the earth, there was only a formless void and the Spirit of God was like a hurricane over water.

Then God said, "Let there be light," and there was light. God separated the light from the darkness so that there was day and there was night. God saw that it was good. Evening came, and morning followed; the first day.

Then God said, "Let there be a sky to separate the upper waters from the lower waters." And so, it happened. Upper waters gathered in the sky and lower waters gathered below the sky, and it was good. Evening came, and morning followed; the second day.

Then God said, "Let the waters under the sky be gathered so that dry land will appear." And so, it happened. The waters gathered into the oceans and dry land appeared. God saw that it was good. Then God said, "Let the earth bring forth every kind of vegetation; plants with seeds and with fruit." And so, it happened. And God saw that it was good. Evening came, and morning followed; the third day.

Then God said, "Let the sun and the moon and the stars and planets fill the sky and let them shine light onto the earth." And so, it happened. The moon and stars were set to govern the night and the sun was set to govern the day. And God saw that it was good. Evening came, and morning followed; the fourth day.

Then God said, "Let the waters teem with life and let birds fly in the sky." And it happened. Fish and whales and creatures of all kind filled the seas and all kinds of winged birds crossed the sky. God saw that it was good. Evening came, and morning followed; the fifth day.

Then God said, "Let the earth bring forth all kinds of living things, hoofed animals, crawling things, and wild animals of all kinds." And so, it happened. Then God said, "Let us make man in our own image and let him have dominion over the earth." God created man in his own image, man and woman. In His own divine image, He created them and blessed them and gave them dominion over all the earth and everything in it. God looked at everything he had made, and it was very, very good. Evening came, and morning followed; the sixth day.

On the seventh day God's work of creation was done. So, God blessed the seventh day and made it holy.

This is how God created man...

From the clay of the ground God formed the body of a man and breathed His spirit into its nostrils, and man became a living being, and the breath of God was man's soul.

Then God made a wonderful garden on a fertile plain which is called Eden. God made to grow many kinds of trees and plants that are beautiful to look at and good for food. A river ran through the garden, and outside the garden the river divided into four branches. The first branch was the Pishon which wound throughout the whole land of Havilah, where there is gold. The second branch was the Gihon which wound through the land of Cush. The third was the Tigris, and the fourth was the Euphrates. In the center of the garden God planted the Tree of the Knowledge of Good and Evil.

God settled the man in the Garden of Eden to tend it and care for it. He said to the man, "You may eat of any of the trees in the garden except the Tree of the Knowledge of Good and Evil which is in the center of the garden. The moment you eat from that tree, you will have doomed yourself to death." God made this covenant with the man so man may choose his own path; be it wisdom or foolishness.

God knew that it was not good for man to be alone. He formed from the ground many kinds of animals and he brought them to the man to name them. Whatever the man called each of them was its name. But none proved to be a good and worthy partner for the man. So, God cast a deep sleep upon him and, while the man slept, God took a rib from his side and healed the place where it had been. He fashioned the rib into a woman, and He presented her to the man.

"At last!" cried the man, "This one is bone of my bone and flesh of my flesh, for out of her man she was taken." Thus, a man leaves his father and mother and clings to his wife and the two become as one flesh.

God said to the man and woman, "Be fertile and multiply; fill the earth and have dominion over it and all that is in it."

The man is called Adam which means "man." The woman is called Eve which means "mother" for she is the mother of all mankind, except for her husband. Adam and Eve were naked, yet they felt no shame.

## The Father of Lies
From the books of Ezekiel, Isaiah, Revelation, and others.

God made beings that are pure spirit, yet they have some powers over the physical world and can affect the affairs of men, and to appear, if they wished, as if they had bodies. They are called Angels which means "messengers." Among these was one who was like the Morning Star; who walked in the presence of God and appeared blameless. And he is called

Lucifer which means "barer of light." But he was evil from the beginning, for God had granted the Angels free will, and Lucifer chose pride and envy.

"I will raise a throne above the stars of God," he said. "I will rise above any height. I will be like God." And this one came to be known as Satan which means "enemy" and Devil which means "slanderer" and Beelzebub which means "Lord of Flies." And like flies to carrion, he drew other envious angels to his cause.

There arose a great battle in Heaven. There was a leader of the good angels who was called Michael which means "Who can compare with God?" Michael and his angels fought against Satan and his angels. Satan and his followers fought but were beaten and there was no place for them in Heaven. So, Satan, who is called The Devil and The Father of Lies, was cast like a meteor from the light of Heaven down to darkness which is called Hell and his followers with him, down to Hell and to the Earth. And to this day they roam the earth seeking to devour the souls of men and women.

**The Fall of Man**
From the book of Genesis

The woman was in the garden near the Tree of the Knowledge of Good and Evil. Now Satan, who is the most cunning of all, was hungry for her soul. He came to her as a serpent. "Did God really say to eat from none of the trees of the garden?" he asked.

"We may eat the fruit of any of the trees," answered the woman, "it is only of the fruit of the tree in the middle of the garden that we may not eat for God says, 'If you eat it, or even touch it, you are doomed to die.'"

"You will not die," scoffed the serpent. "God knows that the moment you eat it your eyes will be opened, and you will know good from evil just like God Himself."

The woman looked at the tree. The fruit looked delicious and she desired to have it because she wanted to be like God. So, she took the fruit and ate it. She offered some to her husband and he ate it with her. Then their eyes were opened, and their innocence was gone. They saw they were naked and were embarrassed, so they sewed fig leaves together to make clothes to cover their nakedness.

In the breezy time of the day The Lord God came to the garden, but the man and his wife hid themselves. "Where are you?" called the Lord.

The man answered, "I heard you in the garden," he said, "but I was afraid because I was naked, so I hid."

"Who told you that you were naked?" asked The Lord. "You have eaten of the forbidden fruit."

"It was the woman!" said Adam, "The woman you put here with me; she gave it to me, so I ate it."

"How could you do such a thing?" asked God of the woman.

"The serpent!" she said, "The serpent tricked me into eating it!"

To the serpent the Lord God said, "Because you have done this, you and the woman are enemies; and your offspring and hers. He will strike at your head and you will strike at his heel."

To the woman God said, "I will intensify your pangs of childbirth. In pain shall you bear children. Even so, your urge shall be for your husband and he shall be your master."

To the man God said, "Cursed be the ground because of you! It shall produce thorns and thistles wherever you toil for food. By the sweat of your brow shall you get bread to eat all the days of your life until you return to the ground from which I made you, for you are dirt and into dirt you shall return."

Then God, in His mercy, made leather clothes for them to cover their nakedness and he sent them out of the garden and settled them to the east of Eden to toil for their food and their clothing and their shelter. At the entrance to the garden He stationed an angel with a fiery sword, so no man could ever return.

So, the man and wife broke their covenant with God, but God remains faithful.

## Cain and Abel
From the Book of Genesis

Adam, and Eve settled east of Eden and had many children who, as the years passed, had many children of their own. These toiled in their fields

7

to raise crops or worked to domesticate animals for food, milk, and clothing. They inherited their parents' attraction to sin for, through their parents' original sin, all kinds of sin entered their hearts. And what is sin? Sin is a word, a thought, or an action done to satisfy our own desires in opposition to the will and love of God. These desires have names. They are Lust, Greed, Laziness, Gluttony, Anger, and the two most deadly are Envy, for it was envy that motivated Satan to tempt Eve and Adam; and Pride, for it was pride that caused the couple to disobey their Lord.

One of Adam and Eve's sons was named Cain, and another was named Abel. Cain was a farmer and Abel, a shepherd. One day, each of them offered a sacrifice to the Lord. God accepted Abel's sacrifice for it was his best animal, but Cain's offering was rejected since it was not his best produce. This greatly upset Cain.

The Lord said to him, "Why are you upset? If you do well, you can yet stand tall. But if not, sin is like a hungry demon crouching at your door, yet you can still overcome him."

But Cain let envy consume him. He said to Abel, "Let's go out to the fields." Abel went with him and when they were alone Cain killed his brother.

Later the Lord said to Cain, "Where is your brother, Abel?"

"How should I know?" said Cain, "Am I my brother's keeper?"

"Listen to me," said The Lord. "Your brother's blood cries out to me from the soil! Therefore, you are banned from tilling the soil which you have reddened with your brother's own blood. If you try to farm again, nothing will grow for you. You will wander the Earth; a restless nomad with no place to call your home." So, Cain roamed the earth as an exile all the rest of his life.

# 2

# You and Your Family, I Will Spare

*God, a Man, and His Family*

*Sing to the Lord a new song; sing to the Lord all the earth. Sing to the Lord and bless His name; announce His salvation every day. Tell of God's glory to all the nations, to all peoples, God's wonderful deeds.*

*Psalm 96*

**Noah and the Flood**
From the Book of Genesis

Year followed year and generation followed generation and as the centuries passed, the minds and hearts of men grew in pride and envy. God saw that the earth had become corrupt and full of lawlessness because all of mankind sought only their own pleasure, no matter what it was.

There was one good and blameless man and his name was Noah. God spoke to Noah and said, "The Earth has become lawless and evil because of the selfish desires of mankind, so I will destroy them and all life on earth; but you and your family I will spare. Make a great ship, an ark. Make compartments in it and make it seaworthy. I will cause a great flood upon the earth that will destroy everything that breathes. But you and your wife and your three sons and their wives will be safe inside the ark and I will make a new covenant with you. Take into the ark one male and one female of every kind of animal so they may live on. And of animals that are clean for sacrifice and for eating take seven of each. Take other food for yourselves and food for all the animals into the ark."

Noah obeyed God and he build an ark nearly four hundred and fifty feet long, seventy-five feet wide, and forty-five feet high with three decks inside.

When all was ready God said to Noah, "Go into the ark with your family and the animals, for you alone in this age I find to be truly just."

When Noah had done as the Lord had commanded, water gushed up from within the earth and heavy rains came and flooded the land and lifted the ark. For forty days and forty nights the rains poured down. Higher and higher the swelling waters rose until they covered even the highest mountains and all breathing things on earth perished. Only Noah and those with him in the ark were left.

For one hundred and fifty days the ark drifted on the surface of the water until the water had receded enough that the ark came to rest upon the mountains of the land of Ararat. Forty days after the ark settled, Noah opened its hatch and let out a raven to see what would happen, but it flew back and forth around the sky, for there was only water. Seven days later Noah sent out a dove, but the dove could find no land on which to rest, so it returned to the ark. Noah waited seven more days and he sent the dove out again. In the evening it returned, and in its beak was a small freshly plucked olive branch, so Noah knew there was dry land somewhere. He waited another seven days and he released the dove again and it did not return. Noah removed the hatch cover and saw that the land was drying.

Noah and his family came out onto dry land and they released the animals. Noah built an altar and sacrificed food animals which he burned up, so the flesh of the animals ascended to the heavens in the form of sweet-smelling smoke which pleased the Lord, and this was a new beginning for mankind and God.

"Be fruitful and multiply," said God to Noah and his family. "All the animals of the earth, in the sky, and in the water are yours. And I make a covenant with you and all the Earth that I will never again destroy the Earth by water. Day shall follow day and season shall follow season unceasingly as long as the Earth lasts. As a sign of my word I set my bow in the clouds so that, when rain comes, my bow will be seen as a reminder and a sign of the covenant that I have established between me and all mortal things, that I will never again destroy the Earth by water."

Of Noah's three sons, Japheth's decedents migrated to Europe, Shem became the ancestor of the people of Asia, and Ham became the ancestor of the people of Africa. There was, in time, much going back and forth, and mankind spread over the whole earth as generation followed generation and century followed century. Those who lived off the land prayed to God for rain and abundance. Those who lived off the sea prayed to God for good and calm breezes. Those who lived in the wild prayed to God for strength for the hunt and for fertility. In time each clan and tribe saw God as their own god and so the one God who brought all blessing became, in the eyes of men, one god who brought rain and another god who brought wind, and another god who brought fertility. And, through the lies of Satan, the minds of men produced gods and goddesses that abounded on the earth, under the earth, in the sea, and in the sky until the very idea of just one god who could rule all the realms and bring all the blessings and all the chastisements seemed an absurdity.

So, the people broke the covenant made through the family, but God remains faithful.

# 3

# Through You, All the World Shall Be Blessed

## *God, a Man, and His Clan*

*The Lord is my shepherd, there is nothing I shall want. You let me graze in green pastures; you lead me to quiet waters; you restore my strength. You guide me in right paths for your name's sake. Even if I walk in the valley of the shadow of death, I fear no harm for you are with me; your crook and your staff protect me.*

*You set a banquet before me in front of my enemies; you anoint my head with oil; my cup overflows. Only goodness and love will follow me all the days of my life; I will dwell in the house of the Lord forever.*

*Psalm 23*

## Father Abraham
From the Book of Genesis

One day, perhaps two thousand years before the birth of the Messiah, God called a man through whom He would make a new covenant with mankind. He was Abram, which means "high father." Abram was born into a wealthy family in the city of Ur which was ancient even in those times. He married a beautiful woman named Sarai. Later they moved with his father and family to the city of Haran, which is in northern Mesopotamia. While living there, God spoke to him.

"Go from this land and from your family to a land that I will show you," said The Lord God. "I will make of you a great nation and I will bless you. I will bless those who bless you and curse those who curse you, and through you all the world shall be blessed."

Abram did as he was commanded. He took his wife and his nephew, Lot, and his wife, their many servants and followers, their many flocks and herds and possessions, and left for the land of Canaan which is at the eastern end of the Mediterranean Sea. Though wealthy, Abram had no children for Sarai was barren.

They went into the land of Canaan and God spoke again to Abram. "I will give this land to you and your descendants."

In time Abram's people and Lot's people could not remain together because their flocks and herds were so large that they needed more land. Abram remained in the hill country of Canaan and Lot moved his people and their herds to the plain of the Jordan Valley and camped in an area near the city of Sodom not far from the city of Gomorrah.

While they were there, northern cities invaded the area, scattering the forces of Sodom and their allies, and taking many prisoners including Lot and his people. A survivor came to Abram in the hills and gave him the bad news that his nephew and his people were now slaves. When Abram heard the news, he mustered three hundred and eighteen of his men and went out in pursuit. After several days they caught up with them north of the Sea of Galilee. Under cover of darkness, Abram and his men attacked, routing the enemy and chasing them for several days, almost to Damascus. Lot and the other captives were freed, and much property was recovered.

When Abram and the people returned to the plain, they were greeted by Melchizedek, king of Salem and priest of the One God. He brought out bread and wine.

He blessed Abram saying, "Blessed be Abram by God the Most High, the creator of heaven and earth; and blessed be God the Most High who delivered your enemies into your hands."

Abram gave Melchizedek a tenth of the spoils, which was the customary portion for a priest in those times. All the people were returned to their homes and the mysterious Melchizedek is heard of no more; but, is not forgotten for he is the forerunner of greatness and a sign of great things to come many centuries later.

God had promised that He would give the land to Abram and his descendants but his wife, Sarai, had given him no children. They were worried that there were no descendants to inherit the land. But the word of the Lord came to Abram one quiet night. God took him outside and said, "Look up at the sky and count the stars if you can. So will your descendants be. I am the Lord who brought you to this land. Know this; to your descendants I give this land from the Ravine of Egypt to the Euphrates River."

After living for years in Canaan, Sarai had born no children and was past the age of childbearing, and Abram himself had grown very old. So, Sarai, according to the customs of those times, gave her maidservant, Hagar the Egyptian, to Abram so that she might bear him children. "The Lord has kept me from bearing children," she said to him. "Take my maidservant Hagar. Perhaps I may have sons through her."

Abram did so, and Hagar bore him a son named Ishmael. But the two women became rivals and did not get along.

When Abram was ninety-nine years old the Lord came to him and said "I am God the Almighty. Between you and me I make a covenant. You are to become the father of a host of nations and the ancestor of kings. I will maintain my covenant with you and your descendants for all ages. As for your part, you and all your male descendants shall be circumcised. This shall be the mark of the covenant between me and my people. I will bless your wife and give you a son by her and he shall give rise to many nations and I will maintain my covenant with him and his descendants."

The circumcision of the flesh; an unchangeable mark at the place which is the source of life, was to be a sign and constant reminder to the people of their covenant with God and membership in God's People. God changed Abram's name to Abraham which means "Father of a Host of Nations.' And Sarai's name was changed to Sarah which means "Royal Woman." The Lord's covenant was not for Abraham and his descendants through

Ishmael but with a son of Abraham and Sarah; a son yet to come, even though they were both very old.

One hot afternoon Abraham was sitting at the entrance to his tent under a large tree when he saw three men approaching. There was something about these men; Abraham felt it. He got up and ran to them and bowed down on the ground before them.

"Please do not pass me by," he said. "Let me have water brought to wash your feet and refresh you. Let me bring you something to eat before you go on your way, for I am your servant." Quickly he told Sarah to make rolls and he had his men kill and prepare a tender, choice steer as well as side dishes. He spread the fine meal before the three visitors and waited like a servant under the tree while they ate.

"Where is your wife Sarah?" they asked.

"Inside the tent," he replied.

"I will return to you at this same time next year," said one of them, "and when I do, Sarah will have a son."

Sarah, who was listening from inside the tent, laughed at the idea that she and Abraham might still have sexual pleasure.

"Why did Sarah laugh?" said the one. "Is anything impossible for God? I will return to you next year and Sarah will have a son."

The three strangers set out and Abraham went with them a while in the direction of Sodom. Two of them went on ahead toward Sodom while the one stopped to talk to Abraham.

"There is a great outcry against Sodom and Gomorrah," he said. "The outcry against their immorality is so great that I intend to see if it is warranted."

Abraham knew the bad reputation of Sodom. His nephew Lot lived in Sodom with his family, and Abraham became afraid for his nephew. "Will you destroy the innocent along with the guilty?" Abraham asked sheepishly, "What if you find fifty innocent people in the city? You would not wipe out the fifty innocent people, would you?"

The one replied, "If I find fifty innocent people in Sodom, I will spare the entire city for their sake."

"I know I am but dust before you," said Abraham, "but, what if there were forty innocent people? Would you destroy them?"

"I would spare the city for the sake of the forty," said the one.

"Please be patient with me," said Abraham, "but what if there were thirty innocent people?"

"I would spare them," said the one.

"What if there were twenty?" asked Abraham.

"I will not destroy it," answered the one.

"Forgive me," said Abraham, "but what if there were ten?"

"For the sake of just ten" he replied, "I will not destroy it."

Then the one left and Abraham went home.

The two strangers reached Sodom at sunset. Lot, Abraham's nephew, was sitting near the city gate. When He saw them, he bowed before them and invited them to spend the night in his house.

Before they went to bed all the men of the city, young and old, came to Lot's door.

"Where are the beautiful men who were with you?" they shouted. "Bring them out so that we may have sex with them."

"Don't do this terrible thing!" said Lot from the door. "I would have you take my daughters before I hand these men over to you."

"Get out of the way!" they replied. "You are just an immigrant and you are trying to tell us natives what to do! Move or we'll do worse to you!"

At that moment, the two strangers pulled Lot into the house and struck the assailants with a bright light, so they could no longer see the door. "Gather your family and get ready to leave this city," they said. "The outcry against this immoral place is so great that we will destroy it."

In the gray light of early morning the angels led Lot and his wife and two grown daughters to the city gates. "Leave at once," they said. "Run for your lives. Do not look back or stop anywhere on the plain until you have reached the hills."

"I cannot run that far," said Lot. "Please, may we go just as far as the small village of Zoar or we will die?"

"I grant you that favor," said the stranger. "We will not destroy Zoar."

Lot and his family ran as fast as they could. They arrived at Zoar just as the sun rose over the horizon. Suddenly, a violent storm of fire and burning sulfur roared down on Sodom and Gomorrah, completely burning the cities and the surrounding plains. Ignoring the angels' warning, Lot's wife turned to look back at the catastrophe and was transformed into a pillar of salt. But Lot and his daughters survived.

Early the next morning Abraham returned to the place where he had spoken with the one. He looked down on the plain where Sodom and Gomorrah had been and saw only dense smoke rising as if from a vast furnace. Sodom and Gomorrah had disappeared.

The Lord did for Sarah as he said he would, and she became pregnant in her old age and bore Abraham a son. Abraham named him Isaac which means "laughter" recalling how Sarah laughed when she overheard the Lord say she would bear a son.

"The Lord has given me reason to laugh," said Sarah. "Who would have thought that old Sarah would nurse a child?"

In time, the friction between Sarah and Hagar had become so bad that Abraham had to send Hagar and her son Ishmael away. This he did only after the Lord had promised him that Hagar and Ishmael would be safe. Ishmael became an expert bowman and lived in the wilderness. In time, Hager got a wife for him from the land of Egypt.

Some years later God put Abraham to the test. "Take your especially loved son," God said to Abraham, "and go to Mount Moriah. There you will sacrifice him and burn his body up to me on a height which I will show you."

Early the next morning Abraham took Isaac with him. He told him they were going to offer a sacrifice. On the third day of their trip he saw the place from afar. He put the wood for the fire on Isaac's back and led him up the mountain while he carried the fire and knife himself.

"Father," said Isaac, "here we have the fire and wood, but we have no sheep for the sacrifice."

"God will provide the sacrifice," said Abraham.

When they reached the place, Abraham built an altar of stones and placed the wood on it. Then he tied up his son and laid him on the wood. He reached for the knife.

"Abraham, Abraham!" came a voice.

"Yes, Lord!" answered Abraham.

"Do not harm your son in the least," said the voice. "I know how devoted you are to God since you did not withhold your own beloved son."

Just then Abraham saw a ram nearby; caught by its horns in a thicket. Abraham took the ram and sacrificed it to God in place of his son."

Again, he heard a voice. "I swear by myself that because you did not withhold from me your beloved son, I will bless you and make your descendants as countless as the stars of the sky or the sands of the beach. They shall prosper and through your descendants all the nations of the earth will be blessed; all this because you obeyed me."

## Isaac and Rebekah
From the Book of Genesis

In time Sarah died and was lovingly buried. When Isaac had grown to be a man Abraham called a trusted servant and told him to go and find a wife for Isaac from among their clan in the North. The servant took ten of his master's camels loaded with gifts and set out. He went to the city of Nahor and, near evening, when the women came out to the well to get water, he made the camels kneel by the well.

"God of my master," he prayed, "give me a good sign. I will stand here by the well and when the girls come out for water if I say to one 'please give me water from your jug' and she answers, 'take a drink and I will water your camels too' let her be the one whom you have chosen to marry Isaac."

No sooner had he made this prayer when Rebekah, a daughter of Abram's cousin, came out with her jug. She was a beautiful virgin. When she filled her jug, the servant came to her.

"Please may I have some water?" he said.

"Take some," she answered, "and I will water your camels too."

The servant watched as the girl went back and forth many times with her jug from the well to the drinking trough until the camels had been watered. Then he gave her a gold nose ring and two gold bracelets; very expensive gifts.

"Is there room in your family's house for me to spend the night?" he asked.

"There is," she said, "for you and your camels." She ran off to tell her family. When her brother, who was the man of the house, saw the gold she was wearing and when she had told him what had happened, he ran out to the well and, finding the servant still there, he invited him into his house. The camels were cared for and the servant was an honored guest at dinner. He told them that he had been sent by their relative Abraham to find a wife for Isaac and he told them all that had transpired at the well. He then gave Rebekah and her brother and her mother costly presents. In the morning, Rebekah's brother asked her if she wanted to go to marry Isaac and she said yes. They prayed a blessing over her and sent her off with two maids in the care of Abraham's servant. Days later, near sunset, they came to where Isaac was staying. He saw her from afar and she saw him. When the servant told her who he was she veiled her face as a show of modesty. They were married, and in Isaac's love for her, he found comfort after the death of his mother.

In time Abraham died and Isaac buried him next to Sarah.

For twenty years Isaac and Rebekah had no children. Finally, God blessed Rebekah with twins. But the children in her womb jostled so much that it worried her. She went to consult the Lord and he answered her saying "Two nations are in your womb; two peoples are quarreling inside you. But one shall prevail and the older shall serve the younger." This was puzzling for, even among twins, it was customary that the younger should serve the older since the older inherited the father's wealth.

When her term was fulfilled, she gave birth to twin boys. The first to come out was reddish with a full head of hair so they named him Esau which means "hairy." His brother came right out, still gripping Esau's heel. They named him Jacob.

## Jacob and Rachel
From the Book of Genesis

Esau grew to be a rugged man and a great hunter, so Isaac favored him. But he was impulsive and shortsighted and prone to anger. Jacob was milder and preferred to remain around the tents. He was clever and handsome, and Rebekah favored him. One day Jacob was cooking a stew when Esau came into the camp famished.

"Give me some of that," he demanded, "I'm starving."

"First give me your inheritance," said Jacob. Then Esau took an oath to give Jacob his inheritance in exchange for a bowl of stew.

When he was forty years old, Esau married but there was little peace in Isaac's family because of the rivalry of the brothers.

In his old age Isaac lost his sight and was blind. He called Esau to him one day saying "I may die any day now, my son. Go and hunt some game and make me a good meal and I will give you my special blessing." This special blessing was the same given to Isaac by his father Abraham; and to Abraham by God; that his descendants will be God's chosen people. Rebekah had been eavesdropping on Isaac and Esau. She knew that Jacob was better suited to lead God's people into the future. When Esau went out to hunt, she went quickly to Jacob and told him "Your father is going to give Esau his blessing after he prepares a meal for him. So, you get two kids from the flock and I will prepare them the way your father likes. Then you bring it to your father, so he will give you his blessing."

"But Esau is rough and hairy while I am smooth skinned," said Jacob. "What if he reaches for me and feels my skin?"

"Just do as I say," said Rebekah. So, after she cooked the meal, she put Jacob in Esau's clothes and took the skin of the kids and covered up his arms. And Jacob went into Isaac's tent.

"Father," he said.

"Which of my sons are you?" asked Isaac.

"I am Esau," Jacob lied. "Sit up so you can eat your meal and bless me."

"Come closer and let me feel you," said Isaac. Jacob came close and Isaac placed his hand on Jacob's arm.

"It is the voice of Jacob," he said, "but the arms of Esau. Are you really my first-born son?"

"Of course," said Jacob.

So, Isaac ate the meal. When he had finished, he gave Jacob the blessing meant for Esau; "May God give you the dew of the sky; grain and wine from the abundance of the earth. Let people be your servants and nations give you honor. Be master of your brothers and may your mother's sons bow to you. Cursed be those who curse you and blessed be those who bless you."

No sooner had Jacob left the tent than Esau returned to the camp and began to prepare the meal. He brought it to Isaac saying, "Please father, eat and give me your blessing."

"Who are you?" asked Isaac.

"I am Esau; your first born." He said.

"Then who was it that brought me a meal?" said Isaac, trembling uncontrollably. "I ate it before you came in and gave him my blessing. Now he must remain blessed!"

"Bless me too, father!' cried Esau.

"Your brother tricked me!" said Isaac. "He already has my blessing."

"He has supplanted me twice!" said Esau. "First he takes my birthright and now he takes my blessing! Father, have you only one blessing? Bless me too." And he began to weep.

Finally, Isaac spoke a blessing. "Far from the fertile fields will you dwell, far from the dew of the sky. You shall live by your sword and you shall serve your brother. But when you have had enough, you shall throw off his yoke."

Angry, Esau decided to kill Jacob after their father died. But Rebekah had known of his plans and warned Jacob.

"Listen," she said. "Esau plans to settle matters with you by killing you. Go to my brother Laban and stay with him until your brother's anger cools."

Jacob set off alone for the home of Laban which was many days journey through rough and wild country. While traveling he came upon a certain shrine of stacked stones and, since the sun had already set, he decided to spend the night there. Taking one of the stones from the shrine, he placed it under his head and lay down and slept. He dreamed he saw a stairway going up to Heaven. Angels were going up and down from Heaven to Earth and back again. Then the Lord was standing beside him.

"I am the god of your grandfather, Abraham, and of your father, Isaac," said the Lord. "I will give to you and to your descendants the land on which you lay. They will be as plentiful as the dust of the earth and shall spread out to the East and the West, the North and the South. In them, all the nations of the earth shall find blessings."

Jacob awoke in a fright and found himself alone. Early in the morning, he took the stone on which his head had rested and stood it up as a memorial. He called the place Bethel which means 'House of the Lord."

Jacob came to the house of his uncle, Laban, who welcomed him warmly. Jacob stayed with Laban and tended his sheep.

One day Laban said to Jacob, "You should not serve me for free just because we are relatives. Tell me what you want for pay." Now Laban had two daughters; the older was Leah and she had lovely eyes. The younger was named Rachel and she was well built and beautiful all over and Jacob had already fallen in love with her.

"I will work for you for seven years if you give the hand of your younger daughter Rachel," said Jacob.

"Better you, a clansman, than an outsider," said Laban.

And so, Jacob worked for Laban for seven years. At the end of that time Laban arranged the wedding. He invited many friends and neighbors and there was a great feast. But that night, he sent his older daughter, Leah into the room with Jacob and he slept with her thinking that she was Rachel. When Jacob awoke and saw it was Leah who he had been with he went straight to Laban.

"Wasn't Rachel supposed to be my bride?" he said, "Why did you do this to me?'

"It is not our custom for the younger sister to be married before the older sister," he said. "Spend your honeymoon week with Leah and then I will give you Racheal if you promise to work for me for another seven years."

So, Jacob, the trickster had been tricked himself. After a week, Laban gave Rachael to him and Jacob took Leah and Rachel and Leah's maidservant and Rachael's maidservant into his house, but his heart was for Rachael.

When God saw that Leah was unloved, though she did all the duties of a wife, he blessed her with a son who she named Reuben. Again, she conceived and had a son who was named Simeon. She then gave Jacob a third son and he was named Levi; and a fourth son named Judah. By this time Rachel had thought herself barren and had become so distressed at not giving Jacob any children that she gave to him her maidservant, so she could give him a son through her. The maidservant conceived and gave Jacob a son and they named him Dan. Later the maidservant gave him another son named Naphtali. By this time Leah was concerned that she had conceived no more children so she gave Jacob her maidservant so she could give Jacob more children through her. That woman bore Jacob two sons named Gad and Asher. Then Leah bore Jacob another son named Issachar. Later she gave birth to another son named Zebulun and a daughter named Dinah. Then God, at last, allowed Rachel to conceive and she bore Jacob a son and they named him Joseph.

After caring for Laban's flocks for several years, Jacob decided it was time to take his wives and children and go home. His good stewardship had made Laban a rich man and Laban made Jacob a rich man by giving him a large portion of his belongings when they parted. So, with his wives, his concubines, his children, his servants, and his large flocks and herds, Jacob headed south to the land of his birth.

Jacob sent messengers ahead to his brother Esau to tell him that he was coming as his servant, and he was rich. Thus, he hoped to gain his brother's favor. The messengers returned telling Jacob only that Esau was coming with four hundred men to find him. Jacob, then, fearing that Esau would kill them all, separated his people into two bands in hopes that, if Esau overtook one band, the other could escape. He then sent the messenger back with ten bulls, forty cows, thirty camels, thirty donkeys, and hundreds of sheep and goats as a present for his brother. Then, under cover of darkness, he sent his women and children across a nearby river for safety and waited alone that night because he knew Esau was close by.

That night a man came to him and the two wrestled. They wrestled and struggled a long time, even until the break of dawn. At last, when the man saw that he could not subdue Jacob, he struck Jacob in the hip and dislocated it.

"Let me go now," said the man, 'since the day has dawned."

"I will not let you go until you bless me," said Jacob.

"What is your name?" asked the man.

"My name is Jacob."

"You shall no longer be called Jacob," said the man. "You shall be called Israel which means 'He Who Prevails with God' for you have contended with earthy beings and heavenly beings and have prevailed."

"Please tell me your name," said Jacob.

"Why should you know my name?" said the man. Then he left.

"I have seen the face of God and lived," said Jacob.

He looked up and saw Esau coming with his four hundred men. As his family watched from across the river he went forward to Esau, bowing low seven times to his brother as he went. Esau, when he saw Jacob, started running forward. He ran toward Jacob and when he reached Jacob, he threw his arms around him, kissed him, and they wept.

The two brothers, having reconciled, lived in the land of Canaan but they could not stay together since they were both now so rich and their flocks needed much land. Jacob settled at Bethel where, years before, the Lord had spoken to him.

At Bethel, the Lord appeared to him again saying, "You shall no longer be called Jacob, but your name shall be Israel. Nations shall stem from you and kings shall be your descendants. This land that I once gave to Abraham and Isaac I now give to you and your descendants."

Later Rachel conceived again, giving Israel his twelfth son who was named Benjamin. But Rachel died giving birth to Benjamin. Jacob set up a memorial stone on her grave and the place is still known to this day. Then, at a very old age, Isaac died, and Jacob and Esau buried him.

## Joseph
From the Book of Genesis

Of all his sons, Jacob favored Joseph, the son of his old age and Rachel's first son. He made Joseph a fine long tunic. Because of this, Joseph's brothers were jealous of him.

Once, Joseph had a dream that he shared with his brothers. "We were harvesting grain and binding the stalks into sheaves," he said. "My sheaf stood tall and your sheaves bowed down before it." He told them of another dream where the sun, the moon, and eleven stars bowed down before him. Because of these dreams, his brothers resented him even more.

One day, when Joseph was seventeen, all his brothers, except Benjamin, were tending their father's flocks far from their home. Jacob sent Joseph to check on them. When they saw him coming, they plotted to kill him and throw his body into a nearby cistern. When Reuben heard this, he talked them into not killing him but just abandoning him in the cistern, and they agreed. When Joseph came up to them, they took hold of him, stripped him of his tunic, and threw him in the cistern. Soon a caravan of traders came by bound for Egypt. The brothers sold Joseph to the traders who took him away to Egypt. The brothers killed a goat and put its blood on the tunic and took the tunic to Jacob telling him that they had found it. Jacob thought that Joseph had been killed by wild beasts and he mourned deeply. His sons tried to console him, but they did not dare tell him the truth about their brother.

Joseph was sold to an Egyptian named Potiphar who was the chief steward to Pharaoh himself. (The word pharaoh means king). But the Lord was with Joseph and he got on well. Potiphar made him his personal attendant and placed him in charge of his entire household. Under Joseph's able administration Potiphar's wealth grew. But Joseph was handsome, and Potiphar's wife tried to seduce him. He refused but she persisted. One day when the two were alone in the house she threw herself on Joseph and he ran away, leaving his tunic in her hands. At that she screamed and ran out to the other servants accusing Joseph of trying to rape her, and she showed the tunic as proof. When Potiphar was told this, he had Joseph thrown into prison.

Again, the Lord was with Joseph and he gained the favor of the chief jailer who put him in charge of the other prisoners. After some time had passed, the royal cupbearer and the royal baker each fell out of favor with Pharaoh and they were put into the same prison as Joseph. One night, each of the two men had a disturbing dream. Joseph noticed their unease.

"What troubles you this morning?" he asked.

They told him that they each had a dream that was bothering them, and they wished someone could tell them what they meant.

"You can tell me," said Joseph.

"Well," said the cupbearer, "In my dream I saw a vine and on the vine were three branches. Before my eyes it blossomed and grew bunches of grapes. In my hand was Pharaoh's cup, so I squeezed the grapes, so the juice ran into the cup and I served it to Pharaoh."

"This is what your dream means," said Joseph, "the three branches are three days. In three days, Pharaoh will pardon you and bring you back into his service. You will once again hand Pharaoh his cup as you have in the past. Mention me to Pharaoh when that time comes, for I have done nothing to deserve imprisonment."

"Let me tell you my dream," said the chief baker. "I had three wicker baskets on my head. The top basket had all kinds of baked goods for Pharaoh, but the birds kept coming and pecking at them. That is my dream."

"This is what your dream means," said Joseph, "in three days, Pharaoh will have you executed. You will be impaled on a stake and the birds will come and peck at your flesh."

Three days later was Pharaoh's birthday. He pardoned his cupbearer and executed his baker just as Joseph had said. But the cupbearer forgot to mention Joseph to Pharaoh.

Two years later Pharaoh had a dream that deeply disturbed him. He called together his magicians and wise men and told them of his dream but none of them could interpret it. Then the cupbearer remembered Joseph and told Pharaoh how Joseph had correctly interpreted his dream and that of the baker. Pharaoh had Joseph summoned. Joseph was taken and shaved and bathed and given good clothes and then he was brought before Pharaoh.

"I am told you can interpret dreams," said Pharaoh.

"Not I," said Joseph, "but the Lord will tell Pharaoh the meaning of his dream." Then Pharaoh told Joseph his dream.

"In my dream I was standing on the bank of the Nile. Up out of the water came seven fat and healthy cows. They began to graze on the grass along the river. After them came seven ugly and scrawny cows. The ugliest cows I have ever seen. They came and swallowed up the seven fat cows and even after they had eaten the fat cows they were still as scrawny and skinny as ever. Then I woke up, but I fell back asleep. I dreamed I saw seven ears of good fat grain growing on one stalk. Then seven ears of shriveled dry grain sprouted up and swallowed the seven healthy ears. No one has been able to tell me the meaning of these dreams."

"Both of Pharaoh's dreams have the same meaning," said Joseph. "The seven healthy cows and the seven fat ears are seven years. The seven scrawny cows and the seven shriveled ears are also seven years. For seven years there will be great abundance in the land of Egypt, but these will be followed by seven years of terrible famine. The famine will be so bad that no trace of abundance will be left in all the land. That Pharaoh had the same dream twice means that God has affirmed what will happen and that it will happen soon.

"Let Pharaoh appoint a wise man to take charge of the land and let Pharaoh appoint overseers to help him. Let them store up all the extra grain in the seven years of abundance so that there will be enough stored up for the people to live on during the next seven years of famine."

This advice impressed and pleased Pharaoh and his advisers. "Since God has made you so wise," said Pharaoh, "I appoint you to take charge of all the land of Egypt. You will be second only to me. No one shall move hand or foot in all the land of Egypt without your permission." With that he took his ring off his finger and put it on Joseph's finger. He had him dressed in the finest clothes and gave him a young woman named Asenath, the daughter of a high priest, to be his wife. Joseph was thirty years old at that time.

Joseph traveled all around Egypt, ordering food to be stored up during the seven years of abundance, and mountains of grain were piled up in the cities and towns of Egypt. In those seven years Asenath gave Joseph two sons; one was named Manasseh which means "God has made me forget my troubles" and the other was named Ephraim which means "God has made me fruitful."

After the seven years of abundance, the famine came just as Joseph had foretold. When the people cried for food, Joseph had the vast storehouses opened and the grain was rationed out. Not only did all the Egyptians come to Joseph for grain but people from distant lands came to him for the famine had gripped the whole world.

Now the famine was also in the land of Canaan, so Jacob sent his ten oldest sons to Egypt to buy grain. Only Joseph's full brother Benjamin remained with their father because he was Jacob's favorite living son. The brothers came before Joseph to buy grain, but they did not recognize him in his fine attire and after so many years. He, however, recognized them.

"You look like spies to me," he said through an interpreter, for he chose to speak to them in Egyptian, so they would not know he spoke their language. "You have come to spy out Egypt's weaknesses."

"No, my lord!" they replied. "We, your servants, have only come to buy grain."

"No, you are spies!"

"My lord," they pleaded, "We are honest men. We are all brothers, sons of the same man in Canaan. We were twelve brothers, but the youngest is with our father, the other is gone."

"We will see," said Joseph. "One of you will go back to Canaan and bring the youngest brother to me. The others will remain here as hostages. Unless your younger brother comes, you will never see your father again." And he had them locked up. But, after three days, he summoned them before him.

28

"Listen to me and you shall live," he said, "for I am a god-fearing man. I will let you go back to your father with some food for your starving families. Only one of you will stay as hostage until you bring me your youngest brother."

"This is the punishment we get for what we did to our brother Joseph," they said to each other.

"Didn't I tell you not to harm him?" said Reuben. "Now we will pay for the wrong we did the boy."

They did not know that Joseph understood their language. When he heard what they said, he turned his back and wept. When he regained his composure, he had Simeon taken away. He had his men fill the brothers' bags with grain and secretly put their money back into the bags. They loaded their donkeys, and the brothers left.

That night one of them opened his bag to get feed for his donkey and he discovered the money in the bag. Then they all opened their bags and found that the money they had used to pay for the grain was inside their bags. They were struck with fear and wondered what God had done to them. When they returned to their father, they told him what had happened, but he was unwilling to let Benjamin go after losing Joseph and now Simeon.

Now the famine had gone on for two years and all the grain the brothers brought from Egypt was gone and their families were starving. So, they asked their father to send them back to buy more grain. At first, he refused, not willing to risk Benjamin. But Judah promised to protect him, so Jacob relented. He had them take honey and resin and others of the best products of the land with them as gifts for the Egyptian official and he had them take extra money to replace the money that had been returned to them the first time.

When Joseph was told of their approach, he instructed his servants to slaughter an animal and prepare a midday feast in his house. The brothers, seeing they were being ushered into the official's own house became afraid and apprehensive, thinking it was a trick. But Joseph's steward reassured them. He had their feet washed and their donkeys fed, and they laid out the gifts on the floor to await Joseph's arrival.

When Joseph arrived, they bowed down before him. He inquired as to their health and they replied that they were well.

"And how is your aged father of whom you have spoken?" he asked.

"He is well and in good health," they said.

"This must be your young brother," he said when eyes fell upon his little brother Benjamin. "God bless you, my boy." With that he felt his eyes water and he quickly excused himself and went into another room to cry. When he had regained control of himself, he washed his face and returned. Then he ordered the meal to commence and they ate. During the meal he took his steward aside and gave him secret instructions.

"Fill each man's bag with grain and put their money into the mouth of their bags," he said, "but in the youngest one's bag also put my silver goblet."

After the meal, all the brothers set out back for Canaan. Joseph's steward went after them and when he caught up with them on the road, he said what Joseph had instructed.

"Why did you repay good with evil and steal my master's silver goblet?"

"We did no such thing!" they said.

"If one of you is found with my master's goblet, he will be my slave."

The brothers eagerly opened their bags to show the steward but when he came to Benjamin's bag, he found the goblet inside. The brothers were horrified. They went back with the steward to plead for Benjamin. When they came to Joseph, they threw themselves at his feet.

"How could you do such a thing?" asked Joseph.

"How can I plead our innocence my lord?" said Judah. "We are guilty men, so we are now your slaves."

"I would not do that," said Joseph, "Only the one who stole my goblet shall be my slave. The rest are free to go."

"I beg you, my lord," said Judah, "let me speak. This boy is our old father's most beloved son. His full brother is dead and this one is the last son of that mother who our father loved. I promised our father that I would take care of him and now if we return without him it would kill him. Please, take me instead as your slave and let my brother go back to our father."

"All my servants leave the room!" ordered Joseph and they did so. He broke down and cried. "I am Joseph," he said in their own language.

The brothers were dumbfounded and stood like statues.

"Come closer to me!" he said. And they did so. "I am your brother Joseph who you sold into slavery, but do not be distressed for I know now that it was God's will. He has used me to save many lives including, now, your own. So, you see, it was not really you who sent me to Egypt, but it was God. Hurry back now to our father. Tell him that God has made me, his son, lord of all Egypt. Tell him this famine will last another five years and tell him to gather all his possessions; and you, my brothers, gather all you families and come back to Egypt where I will settle you." At that he embraced and kissed his brothers and they all wept for joy.

Jacob, called Israel, and his sons and all their families settled in Egypt in the land of Goshen, which is in the Nile delta, and Pharaoh gave them land and they prospered. After some time, Jacob died but not before seeing his lost son Joseph as well as Joseph's sons, his grandsons. He was embalmed in Egypt but then, in fulfillment of his last request, his body was taken to Canaan and buried in his family burial place. Joseph lived to see his own grandchildren and great grandchildren. Before he died, he reminded his family that someday they would return to Canaan, the land promised to Abraham and Isaac and Israel, and he extoled them that, when they do, they bring his bones with them. Then Joseph died, and they laid him to rest, for the time being, in Egypt.

When Israel and his family migrated to Egypt to live with Joseph, they were seventy in number. After some time, they grew into clans, and then into tribes, each based on its founding father; that is, on the sons and grandsons of Israel. They were Ruben, Simeon, Levi, Judah, Issachar, Zebulun, Benjamin, Dan, Naphtali, Gad, and Asher, and Joseph's sons, Ephraim and Manasseh each fathered a clan. As generation followed generation, and century followed century, the twelve tribes grew to over a million people. Though they lived for four hundred years in the land of Goshen under the Pharaohs, they retained their customs and language and were considered foreigners in the land of Egypt. The Egyptians called them Hebrews, which means foreigner or immigrant, and they were also called Israelites since they were all descended from Jacob who was called Israel.

But these later generations turned to Egyptian gods; and so, the clan broke their covenant, but God remains faithful.

# 4

# This is My Name Forever

*God, a Man, and His Nation*

*The law of the Lord is perfect, it refreshes the soul. The decree of the Lord is trustworthy, it gives wisdom to the simple. The precepts of the Lord are right, they make the heart rejoice. The command of the Lord is clear, it brightens the eye. The statutes of the Lord are true and just; more desirable than gold, than a hoard of pure gold; sweeter than honey dripping from the comb. By them, your servant is enlightened; obeying them brings much gain.*

*Psalm 19*

## The Leaving
From the Book of Exodus

A Pharaoh came to power who had never heard of Joseph. The Israelites were so numerous that he assigned them hard work to keep them out of trouble. In their labors they built the cities of Pithom and Raamases in Goshen. But the harder they were oppressed, the more they multiplied so, in time, they were reduced to slavery. But still they multiplied, so the Pharaoh ordered that whenever an Israelite woman gave birth to a boy, he should be killed. This took place about thirteen centuries before the birth of the Messiah.

Now a certain Israelite woman from the tribe of Levi bore a healthy son and hid him for three months. When she could hide him no longer, she put him in a watertight basket and placed it in the Nile River among the reeds. She had her daughter hide nearby to see what would happen to the boy. Soon a daughter of Pharaoh and her maids came to the river to bathe. They saw the basket and in it they found the baby boy. The princess knew this must be one of the Israelite boys, but she took pity on him and did not want him to die. The baby's sister came out of hiding and offered to take the baby to an Israelite woman to be nursed. The princess agreed and so the girl took the baby back to his own mother. After the boy had grown some, his mother took him to the princess. The princess adopted him and named him Moses, so the little Israelite boy was raised in the Egyptian royal family.

One day, after Moses had grown to be a man, he saw an Egyptian beating an Israelite slave. Moses struck the Egyptian so hard that it killed him. Having done this, Moses had to leave the country, so he went to a land called Median. One day he was sitting by a well and seven girls came up with their flock to water them. But men came and chased the girls away and began to water their own flock. Moses chased the men away and watered the girls' flock for them. They were daughters of a priest named Jethro. In gratitude, Jethro gave Moses one of his daughters named Zipporah as his bride. Moses lived happily there for many years, and Zipporah bore him sons.

In time the old Pharaoh died but the Israelites were still oppressed. Moses was getting on in years but was still capable and strong.

One day, while he was tending Jethro's flocks in the desert, he saw a bush burning. As he watched, he noticed that, though it was aflame, it was not consumed but remained green. Moses was amazed and went closer for a better look.

As he approached, a voice came to him from out of the bush. "Moses! Moses!"

"Here I am," said Moses.

"Come no closer!" said the voice. "Remove your sandals for you are standing on holy ground. I am the God of your fathers, the God of Abraham, the God of Isaac, the God of Israel."

Moses hid his face, but the voice continued.

"I have seen the suffering of my people in Egypt and heard their cry. I will rescue them from the Egyptians and lead them to a good and spacious land flowing with milk and honey. I will send you to Pharaoh to lead my people out of Egypt."

"But who am I to do this?" said Moses.

"I will be with you," said the Lord.

"But when I tell the Israelites that the god of their fathers has sent me, and they ask me 'What is his name?' what shall I tell them?"

"I am who I am," said the Lord. "This is what you will tell them: 'I AM sent me to you.' This is my name forever. They will listen to you. When you go to Pharaoh, he will not listen to you, but I will strike Egypt with such wonders that he will have to let my people go."

"But what if they don't believe me?" asked Moses in fear.

"Throw your staff on the ground," said the Lord.

Moses did so, and it turned into a snake.

"Now pick it up," said the Lord.

Trembling, Moses did so and when he touched it, it became his staff again.

"But please, Lord," said Moses, "I am not eloquent. I am not a good speaker. Please send someone else."

"Your brother Aaron will speak for you," said the Lord. "Now, take your staff with you, for with it you will work miracles."

The Lord also appeared to Aaron and told him to meet his brother in the desert. When he had done so, the two greeted each other warmly. They made their preparations and then they returned to Egypt.

Moses and Aaron went to the Pharaoh and asked him to let the Hebrews go out into the desert to make sacrifices to their god. Pharaoh grew angry and refused to let the people go. To keep them even busier, he commanded that they could not receive deliveries of straw to make bricks, but they would have to gather the straw themselves, though their brick quota would not be reduced. Those Hebrew foremen who could not meet their quota were beaten. The Hebrew elders complained to Pharaoh, but he would not listen, so they complained to Moses, blaming him for their predicament.

"Lord," said Moses in prayer, "why do you treat your people so badly, and why did you send me on this mission?"

The Lord answered him saying, "You will see what I do with Pharaoh. I AM The Lord. I appeared to Abraham, Isaac, and Jacob. I made my covenant with them to give them the land of Canaan and now that I have heard the groaning of their descendants, I will fulfill that covenant. Tell the people 'I AM the Lord who will free you from slavery in Egypt. You will be my people and I will be your God, and I will bring you to the land which I promised to your fathers. I AM the Lord.'"

"But I am a poor speaker," said Moses. "How will mighty Pharaoh listen to me?"

"I have made you as a god to Pharaoh," answered the Lord, "and you brother Aaron shall be your prophet. Tell him what I command you and he will speak for you in front of Pharaoh."

Moses and Aaron went before Pharaoh again to tell him to let the people go but Pharaoh refused. Then, upon Moses' command, Aaron threw his staff to the ground and it turned into a snake. Pharaoh called for his magicians. They threw their staffs on the ground and their staffs also turned into snakes, but Aaron's snake swallowed their snakes. Even so, Pharaoh was not moved.

The next day Pharaoh went down to the River Nile to bathe. Moses and Aaron were waiting for him.

They said to him, "The god of the Hebrews sent us to you to tell you, 'Let my people go, but you did not listen. Now you shall know that I AM God.'" Upon Moses' command Aaron raised his staff and struck the water of the river in front of Pharaoh and his servants and the river turned to blood. The fish of the river died, and the water was too polluted to drink. Pharaoh summoned his magicians again and they appeared to do the same thing. So, even though the Egyptians had to dig wells for drinking water, he would not let the people go.

A week later Moses and Aaron returned to Pharaoh saying, "The Lord God says to you 'Let my people go. If you refuse, I will send a plague of frogs upon your land. The river will team with frogs. They will come up into your houses, into your beds, even your ovens and mixing bowls. The frogs will swarm all over you and your people.'"

So, Aaron stretched his staff over the canals and pools of Egypt and frogs poured out and covered the land. Then Pharaoh called for Moses and Aaron. "I will let your people go if you free us from this plague of frogs."

Moses went away and prayed to The Lord and the frogs all died. They were gathered into great heaps. There was a great stench, but the frogs were done. Then Pharaoh, feeling relief, broke his word and refused to let the people go.

Then, Aaron raised his staff and struck the dust of the earth and it turned into gnats that covered the entire land of Egypt and infested men and beasts. The magicians could not replicate this feat and told Pharaoh that it was done by the hand of God. Even so, Pharaoh would not let the people go.

Then the Lord came to Moses again and said, "Tell Pharaoh that if he does not let my people go, I will send swarms of flies over Egypt. They will come upon them and into their houses. The very ground on which they stand will be filled with flies, except in Goshen, the land where my people are. There will be no flies there so that everyone may know that my people are special to me."

Then flies covered Egypt, except for Goshen, just as The Lord had said. Pharaoh called for Moses and said he would let them go but he soon changed his mind again.

Then the Lord told Moses to say to Pharaoh, "The God of the Hebrews says, 'Let my people go! If you refuse me, I warn you, tomorrow I will send a plague upon all the livestock of Egypt and your horses, your asses, your camels, your cattle, and sheep will die. But the livestock of the Hebrews will live." Pharaoh refused, and it happened as the Lord had said it would, but Pharaoh remained unmoved.

Then, following God's instructions, Moses and Aaron took soot from a furnace and, in the presence of Pharaoh, tossed it toward the sky. It turned into fine dust that spread all over Egypt and caused festering boils to form on men and beast, even on the magicians of Pharaoh so they could do nothing. But still Pharaoh would not let the people go.

Then Moses returned to Pharaoh and quoting The Lord he said, "You still refuse to let my people go. By now I could have wiped you from the

37

earth. I have only spared you to show you my power and to make my name echo throughout the Earth. Since you still block my people, tomorrow I will send such mighty hail upon Egypt that has never been seen before and shall never be seen again. Guard yourselves. Bring your animals and people indoors so they may be spared for those that are not sheltered shall die." Upon hearing this, many Egyptians brought their animals and people under shelter, but many did not. Then Moses raised his staff up to the sky and thunder and lightning rang out unceasingly and hail poured down upon the land. Those who were outside died, and many crops and trees were destroyed. Only in the land of Goshen did it not hail.

Pharaoh immediately called for Moses and told him, "Pray to The Lord to stop this hail and I will let you go. You need stay no more!"

So, Moses prayed to God and the storms stopped. But, again, Pharaoh changed his mind and refused to let the people go.

Then the Lord said to Moses, "I have made Pharaoh stubborn so you could tell your children and grandchildren of my power and the mighty things I have done so they may know that I AM God. Go and tell Pharaoh that if he still refuses to let my people go, I shall bring locusts upon Egypt. They shall cover the ground and eat up what has been saved from the hail."

Moses told this to Pharaoh and many of Pharaoh's advisers told him to let the Hebrews go, but he would not. The next day Moses raised his staff and a mighty East wind came over Egypt that blew hard all day and all night. At dawn, the locusts came on the East wind. They covered the land, so it was black, and they ate up every green thing in Egypt. Pharaoh summoned Moses again and said he would let the people go if the locusts were stopped. Moses prayed, and a strong West wind blew up and carried all the locusts away and out over the Sea of Reeds. As soon as they were gone Pharaoh changed his mind again.

Then Moses raised his staff to the sky and a heavy darkness settled over the land. For three days it was so dark that no one could see to move. Only in the land of Goshen did the sun shine.

Pharaoh called Moses again and said, "Go. Take your old ones and your young ones and go."

"We must also take our livestock," said Moses.

This made Pharaoh very angry and he refused. "Leave my presence!" he said. "Do not come to me again. The day you come before me; you will die!"

Then the Lord said to Moses, "One more plague will I send upon Egypt. After that, Pharaoh will not only let you go, he will send you away. I will go through Egypt and the firstborn of this land shall die, from the firstborn of Pharaoh to the firstborn of the slaves, even of the animals. There will be such a cry throughout Egypt that has never been heard before or since. But of the Israelites, not even a dog shall whimper. Tell all the Israelites that on the tenth day of this month every family must procure a lamb. Any families that are too small shall join with other families. The lamb must be a year- old male with no defect. They shall keep it until the fourteenth day of the month, then they shall publicly slaughter it at twilight. They shall take some of the blood of the lamb and spread it on the doorposts and lintels of every house in which the lamb will be consumed. They shall eat its roasted flesh with unleavened bread and bitter herbs. Whatever is left over shall be burned up. This is how you will eat it: you shall eat dressed for travel with your sandals on your feet and your staffs in your hand, like people ready to flee. This is the Passover of the Lord. For on that night I will go through Egypt and strike down the firstborn of the land. But of those houses marked with the blood of the lamb, I shall pass over them and no harm shall come to them. This will become a memorial feast since on this day I brought you out of the land of Egypt. You will celebrate this day every year throughout your generations for all time."

The people did as they were instructed. Each household sacrificed a male lamb in the dim twilight. They used hyssop branches to spread its blood on their door posts and lintels. In the dark of night, they ate its roasted flesh with unleavened bread, with their sandals on their feet and their staffs in their hand. At midnight, the Lord came and took the life of the firstborn of Egypt, from the firstborn of Pharaoh on his throne to the firstborn of the prisoner in the dungeon as well as the firstborn of all the animals. Pharaoh and his servants and all the Egyptians awoke in the night and a great cry rose over all the land for there was not a house without its dead.

Before dawn Pharaoh summoned Moses and Aaron and said "Go and leave my country. Take your families, your herds, and your flocks. Go and you will be doing me a favor."

And all the Egyptians were anxious that the Israelites should go. They gave them their gold and their silver and their fine clothes; whatever they asked for, they gave.

The Twelve tribes of Israelites set out from the city of Rameses: six hundred thousand men with their beloved women and children and with their carts and oxen, their herds, their flocks, and all their possessions. There were many people of mixed blood with them as well as many of other blood; a vast multitude on the move, going to a place they have never seen, by a route they did not know.

The direct road to Canaan was heavily populated and strongly guarded by hostile people so they took a more southerly route toward the desert. The Lord preceded them as a column of smoke by day and a pillar of fire by night. This apparition stayed in front of them always and they could follow it by day or by night.

The Lord led them to camp on the shores of the Sea of Reeds. The sea was between them and their destination. When Pharaoh heard of this, he thought they must be lost and disorganized. So, he mustered his army; six hundred first class chariots and many other chariots loaded with soldiers and sent them after the Israelites. They caught up with them at the edge of the sea.

The Egyptians were already close and coming fast when the Israelites saw their dust. They were trapped between the sea and the Egyptian swords and they did not know what to do. Men were seized with fear and women with despair for themselves and their children.

"Were there no graves in Egypt that you had to bring us out here in the desert to die?" some said to Moses. "Why did you take us from Egypt? Better to be slaves in Egypt than to die in the dessert."

"Do not be afraid!" said Moses to those who could hear him. "Stand your ground and see the victory the Lord will give you today."

The cloud that had been leading the Israelites came around and stood between them and the Egyptians so neither party could approach the other;

and there it stayed. Moses stretched out his staff over the sea and a strong east wind blew up and swept over the sea all night, so, in the morning it was dry land. Moses led the people onto the dry land that had been the sea. In wonder and fear the multitude passed through and the waters of the sea were like walls to their right and to their left. All day long and into the night all the people crossed the sea on dry land. When they had crossed, the cloud blocking the Egyptians lifted, so the army charged into the dry sea on their chariots in pursuit of the Israelites.

Just before dawn, the Lord said to Moses, "Raise your hand over the sea." As the sun rose in the eastern sky, Moses raised his hand and the sea closed in and poured down on the Egyptians. All the Egyptians died that morning. Not a one was left. When the Israelites saw their bodies washed up dead on the seashore, they were amazed. They danced and sang songs and they believed in God and in Moses.

**A New Nation**
From the Books of Exodus, Leviticus, Numbers, and Deuteronomy

Moses led the people out into the desert and by the end of three days they had run out of water. They came to a spring, but it was salty. Some of the people complained. Following God's instructions, Moses tossed a piece of wood into the water and it became fresh. They filled their jugs and moved on.

After traveling for about six weeks they began to run out of food. Again, the people complained to Moses saying, "If we were in Egypt, we would have food, but you have led us out into the desert to die of hunger."

"The Lord has heard your grumbling," said Moses. "In the evening you will have meat, and in the morning, you will have bread."

That evening huge flocks of quail descended into the camp and landed on the ground where they were easily caught. Everybody had their fill. In the morning they awoke to see heavy dew that covered the ground and the whole camp. When the dew evaporated fine flakes covered the ground.

"Manna?" the people asked, which means "What is it?"

"It is the bread which The Lord has given you to eat," said Moses.

They gathered it into baskets. It looked like fine white seeds. When they ate it, it tasted like sweetbread. This bread from Heaven which they called "manna" came every morning. They gathered enough to eat each day and by noon, that which was left on the ground had disappeared. They were fed this way all the time they were in the desert.

In the third month of their travels, they arrived at the foot of the mountain called Horeb, also called Sinai. It was the same mountain where Moses had seen the burning bush and heard the words of the Lord for the first time. At that place, the Lord showed himself to the people in fire and smoke over the whole mountain.

It was the will of the Lord to make a nation of these people dedicated to himself, and through these people He would save all peoples from the tyranny of sin brought into the world by Satan, the Prince of Lies. On His instructions Moses went up the mountain to receive stone tablets containing Ten Commandments which were to be the foundation of the laws of the new nation. Moses brought his young assistant, Joshua, part way up and had him camp there to await his return. Then Moses went on. After Moses had been many days up on the mountain the people began to think he would not return. Forgetting the miracles, they had seen, and being weak of faith, they became confused. So, with the acquiescence of Aaron, they took the gold, which was given to them by the Egyptians, melted it down, and fashioned it into a calf; an idol, a god which they could see like the gods of the Egyptians. They made sacrifice to it and feasted in front of it. Then they held a raucous festival.

The Lord told Moses to go back down to the people, for they had already gone astray from the path He had set them on. On the way down, he met Joshua who told him that a noise like a battle was coming up from the camp. When Moses came down and saw the golden calf and the people dancing in front of it, he grew very angry. He threw the tablets to the ground and they broke. He demanded an explanation from Aaron.

Aaron pleaded with him not to be mad; that the people are influenced by evil and he could do nothing but cooperate.

"Let all who are for the Lord come to me!" shouted Moses. Immediately the people from the tribe of Levi, Moses' own tribe, rallied to him. He had them arm themselves and go through the camp, striking down the rebels, even their own relatives, bringing order back to the camp. They killed about three thousand that day. For their loyalty, the Levites were especially dedicated to the Lord.

Moses had the golden calf beaten into powder. He then had the powder mixed with water and had the people drink it so, by passing though their bodies, it was defiled and scattered over the ground of the desert, never to be used again. He then went back up the mountain to plead for mercy for the stiff-necked Israelites. God showed mercy to those who did not rebel. God rewrote the Ten Commandments on two tablets of stone and gave Moses other laws and rules for the people, for He renewed his covenant with them, though they did not deserve it.

Moses remained on the mountain for forty days and nights without food or water. When he came down holding the tablets, Joshua and the elders saw that his face was radiant, and they were afraid of him. When all the people came to him, they too saw the radiance of his face; so, Moses veiled himself. He gave them the tablets of the Law and he wrote down the laws that the Lord had given him. The Ten Commandments were...

*You shall not have other gods before me. You shall not make statues and images and bow down and worship them.*

*You shall not speak the name of the Lord, your God, disrespectfully.*

*Remember the Sabbath and keep it holy. For six days of the week you may work but on the seventh day, you shall rest.*

*Honor your father and your mother.*

*You shall not kill.*

*You shall not commit adultery.*

*You shall not steal.*

*You shall not bear false witness against your neighbor.*

*You shall not desire your neighbor's wife.*

*You shall not desire anything that belongs to your neighbor.*

By now, the people were pleased to receive the Ten Commandments, and to follow God's instructions. They built an open topped container called the Ark of the Covenant in which to keep the tablets. It was four feet long, two feet wide, and two feet high; made of acacia wood and plated all over with gold. Two gold rings were attached to each side so that long poles could be put through the rings and it could be carried by men holding the poles. The poles were also gold plated. A gold-plated cover was made for it and attached to the cover were two gold statues of angels; one on each end, facing each other, with their wings spread over the box. It was called the Ark of the Covenant because it contained the tablets of the Ten Commandments. It was so holy that no one was to touch it. It was only to be moved by Levites carrying it by the poles. They made a large tent of fine material to house the Ark. The word for tent in Hebrew was "tabernacle." It was forty-five feet long and fifteen feet wide. The Ark was kept at the far end of the tent and a purple and scarlet curtain, embroidered with gold angels, was stretched across the inside, two thirds of the way back, so the Ark could not be seen. The area behind the curtain was called the Holy of Holies. It was where Moses went to consult The Lord. In the Tabernacle, in front of the Holy of Holies, was a gold table with gold cups and plates for sacrificial grain offerings. There was also a beautifully decorated gold lampstand, branching out with seven cups for seven candles. There was a bronze basin for ritual washing and a gold altar for burning incense to the Lord night and day. Outside, in front of the Tabernacle was another bronze washing basin for cleansing oneself before entering the Tabernacle. There was also a bronze plated altar seven and half feet square and four and a half feet high. It was used to burn up the sacrificed animals so they could rise to God in the form of smoke. All of this was surrounded by a perimeter wall of rich cloth; one hundred and fifty feet long, seventy-five feet wide, and seven and a half feet high, all supported by bronze and silver posts spaced seven and a half feet apart. The glory of the Lord would cover the tabernacle like a cloud in the day and like glowing fire in the night.

The keeping of the Ark and setting up, dismantling, and carrying of the Tabernacle and all the holy things was entrusted to Aaron who was made high priest by God and to his sons and the Levites who were the priests. While conducting religious duties and ceremonies, the priests were to wear special robes with a breast plate studded with twelve precious stones, one for each of the tribes of Israel.

Other laws that built on the Ten Commandments were given to this new nation by God through Moses. There were laws so that man might have a right relationship with God. They were, in part…

*Hear, oh Israel! The Lord is our God, The Lord is alone!*

*With a strong hand did the Lord bring us out of Egypt, killing the first born of man and beast. Therefore, the firstborn Israelite male of man and beast belongs to God. The animals are to be sacrificed. But a lesser animal may be sacrificed in the place of a more valuable animal. As for the firstborn son of every Hebrew mother, he shall be dedicated to God but shall not be sacrificed. An animal is to be sacrificed in his place as his redemption from death.*

Every year you shall celebrate the Passover with sacrifices and unleavened bread. You shall celebrate the first of the grain harvest and the first of the fruit harvest. You shall also celebrate the Feast of Booths when your descendants shall set up tents or booths and live in them for one week so they may remember how I led you out of Egypt.

Anyone who wishes may make a burnt offering, or holocaust, to the Lord.

Anyone who wishes may bring a cereal offering to the Lord. They should bake unleavened bread with oil and bring it to the priests. Some, the priests shall keep as food. The rest shall be burned with incense, so it rises to Heaven as a sweet-smelling offering to the Lord.

If someone has sinned, they may make a Sin Offering to the Lord. They shall bring an unblemished male animal from the flocks or herds to the priests at the Tabernacle. The priest shall place his hands on the animal's head then slaughter it and put some of its blood on the altar inside the tent as a sign that the life blood of the animal is given for the people. It shall be completely burned so it may ascend to God as a sweet-smelling offering.

If someone wants to make a Peace Offering to the Lord, they may bring an unblemished animal to the priests at the Tabernacle where the priest shall slaughter it and parts of it shall be burned up to God, but, parts shall be eaten by the offerors and the priests as a meal of peace and reconciliation with God.

*For sacrifices for many people you shall bring a perfectly formed young bull. For a family or a person, you may bring an unblemished lamb or kid. If you cannot afford a lamb or kid, you may bring two doves or two pigeons.*

*Daily cereal offerings will be made by Aaron and his sons since they are the priests and they shall keep a lamp lit in the Tabernacle day and night without ceasing.*

*For your food you may eat animals that chew cud and have cloven hoofs such as cattle, sheep, and deer. But not others such as camel, badger, or pig. You may eat fish with scales but not mollusks or crustaceans. You may eat birds but not birds of prey. You may not eat any animal that has died of itself but foreigners living among you may do so. You shall not eat insects or crawling things. Do not consume blood for it is the life of an animal. Do not touch any dead thing except that which you have slaughtered. If you do these things you have made yourself unclean before the Lord. An unclean person cannot touch anything or anyone that is clean and may not participate in the celebrations of the community. A person must bathe and take sacrifices to the priests to be clean again.*

*Anyone who curses God or blasphemes His name shall be put to death.*

There were laws so that man might have a right relationship with family. They were, in part…

*You shall not sacrifice your children or any other hu-
man. A man shall not lay with a man like a woman
and a woman shall not lay with woman like a man.
A man shall not have sex with a woman during her
menstrual time. You will not have sex with close
relatives or in-laws, and you will have no such re-
lationships with animals. These are abominations
practiced by the people of Canaan, the land to which
I am taking you. Because they have defiled the land
with such abominations, I will make the land vomit
them out and I will replace them with you. If you
take up these practices, the land will also vomit you
out for defiling it.*

*When a woman is having her menstrual flow, she
is unclean and may not be touched. Anything she
touches must be washed.*

*A woman who has given birth shall be unclean be-
cause of her flow of blood. If she has a son, he shall be
circumcised on the eighth day of his life. She shall be
considered unclean for another thirty days and not
be touched so she may heal. After that time, she may
take a sacrifice to the priests and be considered clean.*

There were laws so that man might have a right relationship with community. They were, in part…

*When you harvest your crops, leave some behind, so
the poor and aliens can gather food for themselves.
If someone is found to have stolen anything, they
shall admit their fault and return the stolen items
along with an additional one fifth of its value to the
owner. Do not make fun of the disabled. When you*

*pass judgments, you shall be fair and impartial. Do not practice divination or go to mediums for they will defile you. Stand up in the presence of old people and show them respect. Do not bother aliens who live among you; love them as you love yourselves for you were once aliens in the land of Egypt. Be honest in all your business dealings. You shall love your neighbor as yourself.*

*Be careful to observe all that I have decreed. I AM the Lord. If you live in accordance with my laws, I will make you prosper. I will establish peace and security in your land, and you will sleep soundly without worries. I will make my dwelling place among you. I shall be your God and you shall be my people. But if you reject my laws and refuse to obey my commandments, I will turn away from you. You shall suffer hunger and sickness and war. You shall be helpless against your enemies and shall be disbursed and lost among them. They will beat you down until only a remnant remains and those shall admit their guilt and the guilt of their fathers. But I will not abandon them. I will remember the covenant I made with their forefathers; with Abraham, with Isaac, with Jacob, and with the Israelites who I took out of the Land of Egypt.*

## Toward the Holy Land
From the Book of Numbers

While at Mount Sinai, a census was taken of all the men that were fit for military service and the number was six hundred and three thousand five hundred and fifty. But the men of the tribe of Levi were not counted as they were not for military service but were to perform the priestly duties;

to care for the Tabernacle and the Ark and all the holy objects and to make sacrifices and, while the other tribes were to camp in their own places, the tribe of Levi was to camp around the Tabernacle area.

After two years at the foot of Mount Sinai the cloud rose from the tabernacle. The people broke camp and, with the Ark of the Covenant at their front, they followed the cloud for several days and camped near the land of Canaan. Again, the people complained. Even Moses' brother Aaron and his sister Miriam complained against Moses. Moses had grown sick of the people and he complained to God. God placated the ungrateful people by sending quail to them again, so they could have something besides Manna to eat.

Moses sent twelve men into Canaan to scout it out. Among them were Caleb, son of Jephunneh and Joshua which means "God Saves." Joshua had been Moses' assistant since his youth. After reconnoitering the land for forty days they returned with beautiful samples of the fruit of the land including figs, and pomegranates, and a cluster of grapes so big it took two men to carry it on a pole.

"the land is flowing with milk and honey," they said, "but, the people there are very strong and fierce. They live in well fortified cities and are very numerous. There are also giants in the land. We felt like grasshoppers next to them. We can never take the land."

Though Caleb and Joshua told the people that they could take the land, the people believed their other comrades, and they grumbled and wailed all day and into the night as they had done many times before. "Would that we had died in Egypt or here in the desert!" they cried. "Why did the Lord bring us all the way here just to be cut down by the sword? Our children will be taken away! Let us appoint a new leader who will take us back to Egypt."

Moses, Aaron, and Caleb and Joshua pleaded with the people to have faith and not to rebel against the Lord who has brought them safe so far. In answer, the people threatened to stone them to death.

Then the Lord spoke to the people through Moses saying, "By my life I will do to you just as you have said! Here in the desert shall your dead

50

bodies fall. Of all you grumblers of twenty years or more, not one shall enter the land I have offered you except Caleb and Joshua. But your little ones, who you said would be taken as booty, they shall dwell in the land you rejected.

"As for you, you will die here in the desert where your children must wonder for forty years because of your faithlessness, until the last of you lies dead in the sand. For forty days you scouted the land and for forty years you shall wander the desert for your crimes. I, the Lord, have spoken."

The ten men of the scouting party, who gave such a bad report and stirred such fear among the people, dropped dead.

Then the people were filled with remorse. Early the next morning the fighting men gathered, saying to Moses, "Here we are, ready to take the land. We were wrong but now we will go."

"Why are you disobeying the Lord again?" said Moses. "Do not go. He will not be with you and you will be defeated."

But they went anyway, without Moses and without the Ark. They were met by the Canaanites, who beat them in bloody combat and drove them away.

Years passed, and the people wandered, homeless, in the desert. They raised flocks and ate manna and drank water. They traded with some people and battled with others. They married, worked, and lived as no-mads. In time, Moses' brother Aaron died. His sister, Miriam and his wife, Zipporah died and all those of his generation died and all those who were over twenty years old when they rebelled against God died except Joshua and Caleb, who were now old, and Moses, who was very old. Those who were newborn babes on the day of the rebellion were now forty years old with children of their own. They had become a nation but without a country. The time had come to take the Promised Land.

Moses, knowing that he would not enter the Promised Land, took a scroll and wrote further explanations of the Law which God had given; and he gathered all the people on the Plain of Moab, just across the Jordan River from the Promised Land. There he read to them his final instructions.

He told them that they were to drive out the people living in the Promised Land and to destroy all their sacred places where they worshipped false gods and sacrificed children. He told them that each clan of each tribe will have its own land according to its population, except for the Levites who, because they were the priests, would have their own cities and towns spread among the other tribes. He gave them warnings and encouragement…

"Cursed be he who makes an idol for worship. Cursed be he who dishonors his parents. Cursed be he who moves his neighbor's landmarks. Cursed be he who misleads a blind man. Cursed be he who violates the rights of aliens, or of widows, or of orphans. Cursed be he who lies with animals or close relatives. Cursed be he who kills in secret or for money. Cursed be he who does not fulfill the provisions of the Law.

"But of those who obey the Law; you will be blessed in the city and in the country. You will be blessed by the fruit of your womb, by the produce of the soil, and by the offspring of your animals. You will be blessed in your grain bin and in your kneading bowl. You will be blessed in your coming and in your going.

"These commands I give you are not mysterious or remote," he said to the assembled multitude. "It is not up in the sky or across the sea for you to ask, 'who can find God's law for us?' No, it is near to you. It is already on your lips and in your hearts. You have but to carry it out.

"So, now you have it. If you choose to love the Lord and follow his commandments and walk in his ways, you will live happy lives in your land and so will your children. If you do not follow the Lord and let yourselves be led astray to follow false gods and to live bad lives, you will not have long and prosperous lives in the land. I lay before you life and death, blessing, and curse. Choose life."

The chiefs and the judges and the elders and the officials and the men and women accepted the Law as given to them by God through Moses and the scroll was placed in the Ark of the Covenant, to be kept safe always with the tablets of the Ten Commandments.

Then Moses laid his hands on the head of Joshua and appointed him to be his successor and the people agreed.

Then Moses went up from the plain to the top of Mount Nebo which is opposite the Jorden Valley from the city of Jericho, and God showed him the Holy Land. He saw the Sea of Galilee and the land all around it. He saw, what would be the hill country of, Judea, what would be the lands of Ephraim and Manasseh, all the way to the Mediterranean Sea. He saw the Negev, the Dead Sea, and all the land around. Then God said to him, "This is the land I have sworn to Abraham, to Isaac, to Jacob, and their descendants. I have let you gaze upon it, but it is not for you to enter." So there, in Moab, in sight of the Holy Land, Moses died. He was one hundred and twenty-five years old and still was sharp of mind and of eye. He was buried there, and no one knows where his body rests. For thirty days the people of Israel wept and mourned for him. When they had finished mourning for Moses, they turned to Joshua.

# 5

# God Has Given This Land to You

## *The Nation Takes Root*

*Blessed be the Lord, my rock who trains my hands for battle, my fingers for war; my safety and my fortress, my stronghold and my deliverer; my shield in whom I trust, who subdues peoples under me.*
*Psalm 144*

## The Taking of the Holy Land
From the book of Joshua

The Lord said the Joshua, "Prepare to cross the Jordan here. I will give you every place you set your foot, for this is the land I promised your fathers that their descendants would own. Above all, keep the laws I have given you. Recite them day and night and be steadfast and you will attain your goal. Do not fear for God is with you wherever you go."

Joshua sent two spies across the Jordan to reconnoiter the walled city of Jericho and the land around it. When they passed into the city, they stayed at the inn of a prostitute named Rahab, but the king of Jericho found out about the strangers and sent word for Rahab to hand them over. She told the messenger that the two had been there, but they left. Then she took the spies up on the flat roof of the house and hid them among stalks of flax that had been spread out there to dry.

"I know your God has given this land to you," she said to them quietly. "There is a great dread of you because we have heard how your God dried up the sea when you came out of Egypt, and how you have beaten you enamies in the desert on your long way to this place. Everyone in this land is filled with fear since your god is the god of heaven above and earth below. Now promise me this; since I have shown kindness to you, you will show kindness to me and my family. Protect my father and my mother and my brothers and sisters and all their families that we may not die."

"We pledge our lives to you," they said. "If you do not betray us, we will show kindness to you when The Lord gives us this land."

Then she let them down through her window with a rope since her house was built into the city walls and the window opened to outside of the city. "Go up into the hills," she said. "Hide there for three days until the king's men stop looking for you. Then you can go on your way."

"We will honor our pledge to you," they said. "Tie a red rope in the window from which you have let us down. When we come, make sure your entire family is gathered inside; let no one go out. Everyone who is inside, when we come, shall be safe." Then the two hid in the hills and were not found. After three days, they returned to Joshua and reported all that they had seen.

The next morning, Joshua moved the entire camp down to the bank of the Jordan. After three days of preparation, he sent word throughout the camp saying, "When you see the Ark of the Covenant being carried by the Levites, follow behind it. Sanctify yourselves, for tomorrow The Lord will work wonders."

In the morning, the people struck camp. Now the Jordan River was in flood stage and the waters were wide and swift. But when the priests carrying the Ark waded out into it, the flow from upstream stopped and the water backed up a long way while the downstream waters flowed away. And so, the priests with the Ark remained in the middle of the riverbed while all the people passed by it, crossing the Jordan on dry land. There were about forty thousand troops not counting all the other people. After all the people had passed, Joshua had twelve large stones taken from the riverbed and set up in a circle on the bank and this memorial stood there for hundreds of years thereafter. The people camped there on the West side of the Jordan and, when the priests brought the Ark of the Covenant out of the riverbed, the water flowed again.

The people celebrated Passover there on the plain of Jericho in the Promised Land and on that day the Manna stopped forever, and they ate of the produce of their new land of Canna.

While Joshua was near Jericho, he looked up and saw someone facing him, sword in hand. Joshua asked him, "Are you friend or foe?"

"Neither," he said. 'I am the captain of the army of The Lord. Remove your sandals for you are on holy ground."

Joshua removed his sandals and fell prostrate on the ground in front of him.

"The Lord has delivered Jericho to you," said the man. "Have all your soldiers march around the city; once each day for six days, following the Ark of the Covenant, and ahead of the Ark, have seven priests carrying ram's horns. On the seventh day have your army march seven times around the city. Then have the priest blow a long blast on their horns and have the army give a great shout. The walls of the city will collapse and then your army can enter the city."

Joshua did as he was commanded. Early the next morning he had his army march around the city with the Ark in front of them and a company of his best troops in front of the Ark and seven priests carrying horns in the lead. The army remained silent and did not say a word as they marched. For six days they did the same thing. On the seventh day, they set out at dawn and marched seven times around the city. Then Joshua had the priests blow a long blast on the horns and he had the army give a mighty shout. The walls came tumbling down. The army stormed the city and took it. They took no booty for themselves, but only precious metals and jewels that they deposited in the treasury of the Lord. Nothing else of any value was taken. The prostitute Rahab and her family were spared, and they and their descendants lived among the Israelites for many generations. The city and everything else in it were burned as an offering to the Lord and the news of Joshua's victory spread throughout the land.

Some of the Canaanites left the land to the Israelites, some allied with them, but most would not make peace with them and they joined against them and fought. And there were many bloody battles and many cities were taken. Whenever the Israelites observed the commandments of God, they were victorious; whenever they disobeyed The Lord, they were defeated. After many years, Joshua had captured the central hill country, the Negev to the South, all the lands around the Sea of Galilee, and the lands on both sided of the Jordan River. The tribe of Asher was given the Northern coastal region. Naphtali received the inland area around Mount Hermon. Gad and Reuben settled the land east of the Jordan River. Zebulun, Issachar, and Manasseh settled in the lands to the East and the West of the Sea of Galilee to the Mediterranean Sea. Dan, Ephraim, and Benjamin settled to the South of Manasseh. Judah received the hill country west of the Dead Sea and Simeon settled in the Negev to the South; while Levi had their own cities scattered among the others.

Many years after entering the Promised Land, when Joshua was very old, he summoned the elders of the twelve tribes, and they gathered under a very large oak tree. "As you can see," he said, "I am going the way of all men. So, acknowledge that The Lord has kept his promises. If you keep his laws, you will prosper. If you break your covenant with The Lord and worship other Gods, you will perish from this land which The Lord has given you. Now fear the Lord and serve him completely. Decide now if you will serve The Lord or if you will worship the gods of the Egyptians or the gods of the Canaanites of this land. As for me and my house, we will serve the Lord."

The people answered, "Far be it from us to forsake The Lord who has taken us out of Egypt and given us this land. We will serve The Lord, for he is our God."

Then Joshua instructed them and encouraged them one more time. He had a large stone stood up there under the oak where they met. "This stone is our witness," he said, "for it has heard all that we have said here." Then he dismissed them.

Shortly thereafter, Joshua died at the age of one hundred and ten years.

He was buried in the land of his inheritance in the mountain region of Ephraim. The bones of Joseph, which the Israelites had brought out of Egypt, were buried in the place which his father, Jacob, had bought when he was alive, and it was an inheritance of the descendants of Joseph. And all the time Joshua was alive, and for many years afterwards, the people served The Lord.

## The Judges of Israel
From the Book of Judges

Several Canaanite cities were not taken, for God had allowed some to remain as a test for future generations of Israelites. There were Canaanites, Hittites, Amorites, and Jebusites. These lived not only in their own cities but also, in time, came to live among the Israelites and they even intermarried. Also, a new people had settled in the southern coastal land. These were the Philistines, a war-like people who came by sea from the island of Crete, and they established five strong cities.

In time, many Israelites forsook The Lord, preferring the sexual promiscuity and worldly life of the Canaanites among them. So, The Lord allowed them to fall into the power of the Canaanites of the city of Hazor, and their general was named Sisera and he commanded nine hundred iron chariots among his forces. At that time, a prophetess named Deborah, wife of Lappidoth, was judge over Israel. She organized a rebellion and set an ambush in which ten thousand Israelites ambushed Sisera in a narrow pass where his chariots could not maneuver, and the Canaanite army was destroyed. Sisera escaped and came to the tent of a Canaanite woman named Jael. She invited him in and hid him under a rug. He told her that, when the Israelite soldiers came, she was to say there was no one there. But Jael waited till Sisera fell asleep. Then she got a tent peg and a mallet and crept up on Sisera and drove the tent peg into his temple and all the way to the ground. When the Israelites came, she showed them the body of Sisera with the tent peg through his head. After this the Israelites, having been saved by two women, overthrew the city of Hazor, and the land was at rest for forty years.

Again, the Israelites were seduced away from The Lord, so he allowed them to be oppressed by the Midianites for seven years. When they cried out again to the Lord, He sent an angel to sit under an oak tree where a young man named Gideon was threshing wheat. "The Lord be with you, oh champion!" said the angel.

"If the Lord is with us, why has he allowed us be so oppressed?" said Gideon.

"Where are his great works that our ancestors saw when He led them out of Egypt?"

"Do not worry for I am with you," said the angel. "You will free the Israelites and destroy the Midianites."

"If this is true, then give me a sign," said Gideon.

The angel instructed him to set up an altar of sacrifice. So, Gideon set up an altar and laid meat and unleavened bread on it as according to the Law. Then the angel touched the meat and bread with the tip of his staff, and it burst into flames and the angel vanished.

Convinced, Gideon organized a band of men and together they tore down the shrines to the false god Baal that were throughout the land. They set up altars and made sacrifices to The Lord. In response, the Midianites gathered a large army, which camped in the Jezreel Valley. Meanwhile, Gideon gathered and army of thirty-two thousand men from the tribes of Israel and camped in the mountains above the valley. The Lord came to Gideon and said, "You have too many soldiers. If you defeat the Midianites with this many men, the people will think that it was them, and not I, who brought the victory. In the morning, let all those who are afraid go home." So, Gideon dismissed those who wish to go and twenty-two thousand left, but ten thousand remained. "It is still too many," said The Lord. "Lead them to the river to drink. Those who bend down to drink with their mouths you will set to one side. Those who bring the water up to their mouths in their hands you will set to the other side." When this was done, those who brought the water up to their mouths numbered three hundred. "By these three hundred you will save Israel," said The Lord. The rest were dismissed.

In the dark of the night, Gideon led the three hundred down toward the Midianite camp. Each of the three hundred had a horn and a jar with a flame inside it. Gideon had split them up into three companies and told them that, at his signal, each man was to break his jar and hold the flame high while blowing his horn and shouting "A sword for The Lord and Gideon." When the three companies had surrounded the Midianite camp Gideon broke his jar and held his flame up and shouted and blew his horn and all three hundred men did the same. The Midianites thought that the Israelites were in among them. They ran about the camp killing each other in the dark hoping to save their own lives. They fled in disorder in the direction of Midian and, over the next few days, the men of the tribes of Israel harassed and attacked them as they fled, killing them and their leaders. Under Gideon the Israelites went on the offensive and subjugated Midian.

In time the Israelites offended the Lord again, so he allowed them to be subjugated by the Philistines for forty years. Now there was a young man of the tribe of Dan named Sampson. He was a Nazarite, which means Consecrated One. Nazarites were to live especially holy lives and a part of their lifestyle was to drink no alcohol nor to cut their hair. Sampson was hansom and very strong, but he was not wise.

In a town called Timnah, Sampson saw a Philistine woman and desired to marry her. His parents were unhappy that he had not chosen an Israelite woman, but they relented. Sampson accompanied is parents to Timnah to arrange the marriage. While he was alone in a vineyard there, a young lion attacked him, but he killed the lion with his bare hands and tore it to pieces like a kid goat. He told no one of this. They arranged the marriage and left. Later, when they returned to Timnah for the wedding, Sampson saw that a colony of bees had built a hive in the carcass of the lion. He took some honey out of the hive and ate it and shared it with his parents though he did not tell them where it came from. At the wedding feast Sampson proposed some sport to thirty of the Philistine men who were there.

"Let me propose a riddle," he said. "If you solve it within the seven days of the wedding feast, I will give you each a tunic. If you don't, each of you will give me one tunic." The men agreed, and Sampson continued. "Out from the eater came forth food, and out of the strong came sweetness."

The men could not determine the answer so, after three days, they asked Sampson's new wife to get the answer for them. She begged and cried and coaxed Sampson so much that on the seventh day he told her.

The men then came to Sampson to solve the riddle. "What is sweeter than honey, and what is stronger than a lion?" they said.

"If you had not plowed with my heifer, you would not have solved the riddle!" said Sampson. He stormed away and went out and killed thirty Philistine men and took their tunics. He returned and gave them to the thirty men. Then he returned to Israelite country leaving his wife behind.

Months later, around harvest time Sampson returned for his wife but was told that her father had given her to his best man as a wife. In anger Sampson caught three hundred foxes. He tied burning torches to their tales and set them loose in the Philistine wheat fields and the fields all burned. When the Philistines found out who was responsible, they took Sampson's wife and her family and burned them to death. At this Sampson killed many of the Philistines then fled.

The Philistines sent a small army into Israelite territory to get him. They forced the Israelites to hand him over. The Israelites bound him tightly and awaited the Philistines. When the Philistines arrived, they taunted Sampson. As they did so his bonds fell away. He got hold of the jawbone of a donkey that was nearby and with it he killed a thousand Philistines and kept his freedom.

Later Sampson fell in love with a woman named Delilah. She was in league with the Philistines. They told her to find out from Sampson from where his great strength came. So, she asked him how he could be bound and made helpless.

"If you bind me with seven wet bow strings, I will be helpless," he said.

So, the Philistines gave her seven wet bow strings and hid while she bound Sampson in his sleep. "Sampson!" she shouted, "The Philistines are here." With that Samson awoke and broke the bow strings like thread.

"You mocked me and lied to me," she said to him. "Now tell me the truth."

"If you bind me with new and unused rope I will be as helpless as any other man," he said.

61

So, she bound him with new rope and shouted "Sampson, the Philistines are upon you!" And he snapped the rope like thread. Again, she acted indignant and asked him how he could lose his strength. "If you bundle up my long hair with a stick I will be as weak as any other man." As he slept, she bundled his hair and shouted that the Philistines were present. But he undid his hair and was as strong as ever.

She vexed him and bothered him so much that he finally gave in and told her the secret of his strength. "If my hair is cut off, I will be as strong as any man." She saw that he was sincere, so she called the Philistines to their house and, while Sampson slept on her lap, one of them cut off his hair. Then he awoke, and they tied him up and mistreated him, the men as well as Delilah. They took him away and gouged out his eyes.

The Philistines held a great assembly in the temple of their god Dagon to thank Dagon for delivering the hated Sampson to them. As all the lords and ladies of the Philistines were assembled and about three thousand people looked down from the temple roof, they led Sampson out so the whole crowd could see and mock him. Sampson became aware that he was standing between the two strongest pillars of the temple. He stretched out his arms to feel the stone of the pillars. Then he shouted "O Lord remember me! Give me strength one last time and let me die with the Philistines!" Then, with one hand on each pillar, he pushed hard, and the pillars gave way and collapsed, and the sides and roof of the temple fell on Sampson and on the Philistines and he killed more Philistines that day than during his whole life before that.

Sampson's people came down and got his body and buried it in his family's grave site. He had judged Israel for twenty years.

The Israelites enjoyed a respite from the depredations of the Philistines but during these times there was no king in Israel and every man did what he thought was best. So, lawlessness and division arose. Clan fought clan and tribe fought tribe for they were disunited. And many Israelites suffered and died at the hands of their own people.

And so, the nation broke its covenant, but God remains faithful.

# 6

# There, Said the Lord, Anoint That One

*God, A Man, and His Kingdom*

*Oh lord, give your wisdom to the king; your justice to the son of kings; that he may rule your people with justice, your oppressed with fairness, that the mountains may yield their bounty for the people, and the hills give abundance, so he may defend the oppressed, save the poor, and crush the oppressor.*

*Psalm 72*

**The Kingdom**
From the First and Second Books of Samuel

Ever since Joshua took the Holy Land, the Ark of the Covenant had been kept in its tabernacle in the town of Shiloh. There was a young man named Samuel who served in the tabernacle. One night he was asleep in the tabernacle near the Ark and heard his name being called. Samuel awoke "Here I am,' he said. But he was alone. He went to where the priest was sleeping. "Here I am," he said.

"I did not call you," said the priest. "Go back to sleep." So, he did, but he heard his name again. He went back to the priest's room.

"You called me. Here I am."

"I did not call you," said the priest, "go back to sleep." So, he did, but again, he was called and again he went to the priest.

"Here I am. You called me."

But now the priest understood. He told Samuel to go back to sleep and, if he is called again to say, "Speak Lord, I your servant am listening." Samuel went back to sleep and heard his name again.

He said, "Speak Lord, I your servant am listening." And the Lord spoke to Samuel for the first time, telling him of things to come.

Samuel matured, and the people could see that The Lord was with him and he became a prophet among all the people of Israel. And Samuel continued to serve The Lord at Shiloh.

By that time, the Philistines had regained their strength and they sent an army to invade Israel. They defeated the Israelites and captured the Ark of the Covenant. They took it back to their country as a trophy and placed it in the temple of Dagon in the city of Ashod. But the statue of Dagon fell in the night and broke and the people were afflicted with hemorrhoids and with a plague of mice. Then the Ark was moved to another city. But the same misfortune befell that city, so it was moved to another city where the same thing happened. After being moved from city to city the Philistines placed the Ark in a cart and sent it back to the Israelites. The Israelites received the Ark with rejoicing. They turned back to the Lord and became more religious.

At Samuel's command the Israelites gathered at a place called Mizpah to pray and ask forgiveness of The Lord. The Philistines heard of the gathering, so they sent an army to attack them. The Israelites were afraid, but Samuel prayed to the Lord and The Lord gave them a great victory over the Philistines.

When Samuel was an old man the people of Israel began to ask that God provide them with a king to unite them. The Lord told Samuel to grant the people what they asked, so Samuel went in search of a king for Israel. Eventually it was decided that a certain tall and strong man would be the king and Samuel anointed him, and the people accepted him, and his name was Saul. Saul brought victory in battle to the Israelites and he ruled with strength. But Saul ruled unwisely and was not obedient to The Lord, so The Lord revealed to Samuel that another would take Saul's place.

The Lord commanded Samuel to fill his horn with oil and travel to the town of Bethlehem, to the house of a man named Jesse, for the Lord had chosen the future king of Israel from among Jesse's sons. The town leaders and their best men came out to greet Samuel and they sacrificed to The Lord and feasted. Samuel had Jesse call his sons over, one by one, to be presented to him. When Samuel saw how hansom and strong the first son was, he thought that this must be the one. But the Lord said to him, "Do not be fooled by his appearance. I have not chosen him. God does not see as man sees, for man sees the appearance, but God sees the heart." So, Jesse brought his second son, but The Lord rejected him. One at a time, then, seven sons were presented to Samuel and none was chosen.

"Have you no more sons?" asked Samuel.

"There is the youngest one," said Jesse, "He is out tending the sheep."

"Send for him" said Samuel. When he came, Samuel saw the lad was hansom and ruddy, making a good appearance. "There," said The Lord, "Anoint that one." Samuel anointed the young man, pouring oil over him in the presence of his brothers. And from that day on, the Spirit of The Lord was upon the young man. And his was David.

Now, Saul had lost favor with God and became subject to moods of depression. One of Saul's servants knew that David, the son of Jesse of Bethlehem, could play the harp and was also a good speaker and a strong lad. So, Saul sent for him and when Saul fell into a bad mood, David played his harp and Saul was soothed. Saul took David into his service.

Not long after that, the Philistines invaded the land. Saul gathered his forces and went out to do battle. The two armies camped on two hills with a valley between them.

When the armies had lined up for battle a Philistine champion named Goliath came forward to challenge the Israelites. He was a giant of a man with a bronze helmet, bronze armor, a long bronze sword, and a heavy spear with an iron tip. "Why are you lined up for battle?" he shouted,

"Send you best man to fight me! If he kills me, we will be your servants, but if I kill him you will be our servants. Well? I defy you! Send me a man to fight!"

The Israelites were afraid of Goliath and no one came forward. Even when Saul asked for a volunteer, no one spoke up. For forty days the armies camped across the valley and each morning and each evening the giant came out, issued his challenge, but no one answered him.

Meanwhile, David was tending his father's sheep, but his three oldest brothers were in the army with Saul. Jesse sent David to bring some food to his brothers in the army. While David was in the camp, Goliath came out and issued his challenge, but no one answered.

When David saw how Goliath taunted the Israelites, he grew angry. He went to Saul and said "Let your majesty not lose heart. I, your servant David, will fight Goliath."

"You cannot go up against that giant," said Saul, "You are a youth while he has been a warrior all his life."

"I have tended my father's flocks for a long time," said David. "When a lion or bear would come, I would chase it and take the sheep right out of its mouth. If they attacked me, I killed them. I have killed a lion and I have killed a bear; I can kill that foreigner too. The Lord has protected me against lions and bears, and He will protect me from the Philistine."

Saul was impressed with his spirit. "Go then," he said, "The Lord will protect you." Then Saul had David dressed in his own armor and gave him his own sword and shield.

"I can't wear these," said David "I am not used to them." He took them off. He went to the creek and found five smooth round stones which he put into his shepherd's bag and, with his staff in one hand and his sling in his other hand, he went out to face Goliath.

When Goliath saw David, he laughed. "Am I a dog that you come at me with a stick?" He scowled, "Little man, I curse you by all my true gods. Come here then, and I will leave your flesh for the vultures and dogs!"

But David answered, "You come to me with a sword and spear, but I come to you with the power of God. I shall kill you and cut off your head and leave your flesh and the flesh of your whole army for the vultures and dogs, and the whole land shall know that Israel has a God and he does not need swords or spears!"

Goliath advanced on David, but David ran quickly toward Goliath. He took a stone from his bag, fixed it into his sling, and flung it. The stone struck Goliath in the middle of his forehead and he fell to the ground. David ran up and took Goliath's sword. He raised it high and struck off Goliath's head.

When the Philistines saw that their champion was dead, they turned and ran. The army of the Israelites pursued them and cut down all they could, so the bodies of the Philistines lay scattered for miles over the land. The Israelites took all their booty and returned to Saul, and with them was David carrying the head of Goliath. Saul rewarded David by making him commander of his soldiers.

Soon a saying arose among the people; "Saul has killed his thousands, and David his ten thousands!" This made Saul jealous and he began to worry that David would take his kingship.

One day Saul fell into a rage and David began to play the harp for him, but Saul grabbed a spear and flung it at David, hoping to pin him to the wall, but David escaped. Saul showed false good will toward David; giving him his daughter Michal in marriage. He then sent him out to raid the Philistines, secretly hoping that the Philistines would kill him. But wherever David and his men went they were victorious, and his renown grew. One night, Saul sent men to David's house to arrest him, but Michal knew of her father's anger and she warmed David and he fled.

David and some of his men escaped to the wilderness but Saul took many soldiers and went looking for him. One day, David and his men were hiding in a cave while Saul and his men were in the canyon just outside the cave, though they did not know that David and his men were in the cave. Saul went into the cave to relieve himself. When they saw him coming David and his men settled back into the dark recesses of the cave and Saul did not know they were there. While Saul was relieving himself, David silently crawled over to Saul and cut off a piece of his cloak. Saul left the cave and began to move on, but David came out and shouted to him. "My lord and king! See how today the Lord has delivered you to me but I will not raise a hand against my king, for he is the Lord's anointed one and like a father to me." Then he raised the piece of Saul's cloak. "See how I could have killed you but did not. Know then that I plan no harm to you and no rebellion." Then Saul was sorry. "My son!" he said. And the two were reconciled.

Shortly after this Samuel died and all Israel gathered to mourn him, and they buried him at his home in Ramah.

## David
From the First Book of Kings and the First Book of Chronicles

Now David grew in power and prestige. He took other wives and his allies grew in number. Saul's jealousy returned, and he again attempted to destroy David. But war broke out and the Philistines defeated Saul's army. Saul killed himself, rather than be captured. The tribes of Israel accepted David as their king, as Samuel had foretold. David led the army and took the city of Jerusalem, making it is capital. He took more wives and made more alliances, making Jerusalem secure and prosperous.

David assembled thirty thousand of the best men of Israel and went out to get the Ark of the Covenant and bring it to Jerusalem. They made a great procession and the people came out of the city singing and playing musical instruments and blowing horns. As the cart carrying the Ark of the Covenant approached the city, David went before it; leaping and dancing for joy as all the people celebrated. The Ark was brought into the tent David had prepared for it and David offered sacrifices, both sin offerings and peace offerings. All the people came out and David had them all fed in celebration.

Some time later David went to the prophet who had succeeded Samuel. His name was Nathan. David said to Nathan, "Here I am, living in my palace while the Ark of the Lord is in a tent."

The next day Nathan told David what the Lord had said in a dream. "So says The Lord: 'Should you build me house to dwell in? I have been in a tent since the days I brought your ancestors out of Egypt and in all that time have I ever demanded to dwell in a house? It was I who took

68

you from the pastures with you flocks and made you king of Israel. I have been with you always and I have destroyed all your enemies before you. I will make you great and I will fix a place for my people so they may live in security. It is I who will establish a house for you, and when your time on Earth is done, I will raise up your house through your heir and make his kingdom firm. He shall build a temple for me and he shall be like a son to me. When he does wrong, I will chastise him, but I will never withdraw my favor from him as I did Saul. Your house and your kingdom shall endure forever before me.'"

When David heard this he went before the Ark of the Covenant to pray and said, "Who am I, Lord, and who are the members of my house that you have brought me to where I am now? Yet you have told me of my house for years and years to come. What can I say? You are so great my Lord God! There is none like you. You have shown your power through you people, Israel; taking them out of Egypt and cleared this land for them. And now, because you have said so, the House of David, your servant, shall be blessed forever."

David grew in success. He went out with his armies and defeated the Philistines. He defeated the Ammonites who lived in the area and he defeated their allies, the Arameans, and made them subject to him. Though there was still trouble with some of the neighboring kingdoms, most of Israel was prosperous and David was secure in his palace in the new capital of Jerusalem.

One spring, David sent his generals out to war, but he remained in Jerusalem. He was walking on the roof of his palace one evening and, looking down from that height, he saw a woman bathing on her roof top, and she was beautiful, and he wanted her. He found out that her name was Bathsheba and she was the wife of Uriah the Hittite who was an officer in his army and was away at war. David sent for her and she came to him and they laid together. Several days later she sent word to him that she was pregnant.

David sent for Uriah to come to Jerusalem to report how the army was doing. When Uriah had made his report, David told him to go home and relax for a while, thinking that he would lay with Bathsheba and later think that the child was his. But Uriah did not go home. He spent that night with the other officers. The next evening David called him into the palace and asked him why he did not go home to enjoy his wife."

"How can I do that while my comrades are camped and at war?" said Uriah. So, David got him drunk and sent him home again to be with his wife. But he still slept at the barracks.

The next day, when David saw that Uriah was not about to sleep with his wife, he sent him back to the war and gave him a sealed letter to take to the general. The letter said to place Uriah in the front of the line and make an assault, and when the fighting got heavy to pull back and leave Uriah to be killed by the enemy. The order was obeyed, and Uriah was killed in battle.

After Bathsheba had mourned her husband for the proper time, David took her into the palace and made her his wife and she bore him a son.

Then, Nathan, the prophet, came to David. "I need you to pass a judgement," He said. "In a certain town there is a very rich man with much land and very many sheep and cattle. In the same town there is a poor man who had only one ewe lamb. He had bought the ewe lamb with what little money he had and raised it and cared for it. It ate from his table and drank from his cup and slept on his lap. One day a visitor came to the rich man and the rich man wanted to prepare a meal for his visitor. But instead of taking from his own large flocks he took the ewe lamb from the poor man and made a meal of it."

Upon hearing this David said, "That rich man deserves to die! He must repay the poor man four times over because he had no pity for the poor man."

"That man is you!" said Nathan, "So the Lord tells you this: 'I anointed you king of Israel. I rescued you from Saul. I gave you a king's house and a king's wives for yourself. Was that not enough? Why did you do such an evil thing? You have taken Uriah's wife and caused his death by the sword. Therefore, the sword will never leave your house. There will be discord and trouble because of what you have done. You have done your evil in secret, but I will make you punishment to be seen by all.'"

Now David was struck with shame. "I have indeed sinned against The Lord."

Nathan said "The Lord has forgiven you. You shall not die, but since you have so offended The Lord, your child shall die and be taken from you by The Lord."

Thereafter David was plagued by wars from without, and plots and rebellions from within. Yet he did his best to serve The Lord and The Lord did not forget his promises to David. In time The Lord gave David victory over all his foes. Bathsheba remained David's favorite and she bore him a legitimate son and named him Solomon. David grew old. He died peacefully uttering these words, "Is my house and line not firm? God has made an eternal covenant with me; set and secure. He will bring forth all my salvation and all my desires."

## Solomon
From the First Book of Kings and the Fist Book of Chronicles

Solomon, son of David, became king and sat on the throne of his father. His rule was secure, and he allied with Egypt by marrying a daughter of the pharaoh. He built a temple in Jerusalem to house the Ark of the Covenant as Nathan had predicted. He also built a great palace and a new wall around the city.

Solomon went to the pilgrim shrine at Gibeon to make sacrifices to The Lord. While he was there The Lord came to him in a dream and said, "Ask me what you will, and I will grant it."

Solomon answered, "You have shown favor to my father and to me. But I am young and don't know how to govern such a large kingdom. Grant me wisdom so I can judge and rule well."

The Lord said' "Since you did not ask for wealth or glory or long life, I grant your request and I will give you these other things as well. I give you wisdom and wealth and glory and, if you remain faithful to me, I give you long life." When Solomon awoke, he went back to Jerusalem and offered sacrifices before the Ark of the Covenant and gave a feast for all his servants.

One day two women came before Solomon. "My King," said one, "This woman and I live in the same house. I bore a child in that house. Three days later she too bore a child. This woman's child died in the night when she lied on him and smothered him. In the night she took my child from my bed and laid the dead child beside me. When I awoke to nurse my child, I found him dead, but when I looked closely, I saw it was not my child."

"Not so!" said the second woman, "The living son is mine; the dead one is hers."

"No!" said the first woman, "The living one is mine."

"One claims the child is hers, the other claims the child is hers," said the king. "Bring me a sword." When the sword was brought, he said, "Cut the child in half and give each woman an equal share."

"No!" said the first woman, "Do not kill my child, I beg you! Let her have him!"

The other woman said, "It shall be neither mine nor yours, go ahead and divide it."

"Give the child to the first woman and by no means harm him," said the king, "she is his real mother."

When the people of Israel heard of this they marveled because they saw how God had given Solomon such wisdom.

In the fourth year of Solomon's reign, and the four hundred and eightieth year since the departure of the Israelites from Egypt, the construction of the temple of The Lord began in Jerusalem. Solomon had employed thirty thousand men to transport cedar wood from Lebanon and eight thousand stone cutters and eighty thousand workers to transport massive cut stones from the mountains for a huge foundation for the temple. The temple was ninety feet long, thirty feet wide, and forty feet high. The vestibule ran its full width and was fifteen feet deep. Along the sides of the temple were annexes several stories high. The temple was made of finely cut stones and roofed with cedar rafters. The interior walls were cedar paneling from floor to ceiling. Carved into the paneling were flowers, palm trees, and angels and they were all covered over with pure gold. A gold covered cedar partition wall that stretched the full width and height of the interior was placed sixty feet from the entrance, so the back thirty feet were separate from the front sixty feet. This back area was The Holy of Holies where the Ark of the Covenant was kept. The Holy of Holies was a thirty-foot cube, all covered in gold. In it were two gold covered statues of angels with their wings outstretched to fifteen feet high and fifteen feet wide so that one wing of each angel touched the side wall while the other wing touched the tip of the other angel's wing, and those inner wings were over the Ark of the Covenant which rested between the two angels. Only the high priest entered the Holy of Holies, once a year to perform rituals of praise. In front of the entrance to the Holy of Holies was a gold covered altar for burning incense. The floor of the temple was of cedar planks overlade with gold. The doors to the temple were carved over with angels, flowers, and palm trees and covered with gold. Two bronze columns were placed, one on either side of the entrance. They were twenty-seven feet high and six feet in diameter with two hundred bronze pomegranates adorning the sides of each of them. A seven-foot bronze capital in the shape of a lotus flower was on top of each column. In the paved courtyard in front of the temple was the altar where sacrificed animals were burned, transformed into smoke that ascended to the heavens as an offering to God. It was made of bronze and was thirty feet square to hold all the offerings that the crowds would bring to be given to God at the hands of the priests. It rested on a fifteen-foot stone platform so the people could see their offerings being made on their behalf. A large bronze basin was in the courtyard. It was where the priests washed after making the sacrifices. It was seven and a half feet high and fifteen feet in diameter and it rested of twelve bronze ox statues. Several smaller bronze basins were made. These were for the washing of the animal parts that were to be eaten by the offerors who made Peace Offerings, a meal with God. These basins sat on stands made in the images of lions, bulls, and angels. There were also candle stands, incense stands, bowls, and utensils; all made of precious metals. The temple took seven years to construct.

When the temple was completed all the elders and many of the people gathered round to witness the Ark of the Covenant being carried into it by the priests while the Levites played music and sang songs of praise to God. Solomon offered many prayers and very many sheep and oxen were sacrificed as offerings to The Lord and placed on the altar. Then fire came down from heaven and consumed the sacrifices, dazzling all the people. King Solomon offered twenty-two thousand oxen and one hundred and twenty thousand sheep as sacrifices for the dedication of the temple. People would come from all over the land to Jerusalem to make sacrifices in the temple, especially at feast days such as Passover.

Over the next twenty years Solomon established trade relations with many lands, near and far. He built monuments and cities and increased the size of his nation. Gold flowed into his country through trade and tribute to the amount of nearly forty thousand pounds a year. The kings of the earth sought audiences with Solomon to hear his wisdom. When the queen of Sheba heard of Solomon's wisdom, she came to Jerusalem to test him with various questions. She led a great retinue and a great train of camels loaded with spices, gold, and precious stones. When she had seen his wealth and heard his wisdom she said, "Happy are your men and your servants who stand before you every day and hear your wisdom. Blessed is the Lord and blessed is Israel for the Lord has loved her so that He has made you king over her." They exchanged many costly gifts and later she returned to her own country.

It was customary in those times that, when kings made alliances, one king would send another his daughter or niece as a bride, thus uniting the families. Accordingly, Solomon had hundreds of wives. Though he had so many, he loved each dearly and wanted to please them. Many of them were from foreign lands with foreign gods. In his old age Solomon grew week to the desires of his wives and he set up temples and shrines to their gods, so they could worship and sacrifice according to their traditions. This was against the command of God which said that, although foreigners were to always be welcome, only The Lord God was to be publicly worshipped.

Since, in his old age, Solomon showed preference to his wives over the Lord, the Lord told him, "Since you have not kept my covenant and disobeyed me, I will deprive your son of the kingdom. For your father's sake I will not deprive you and I will allow your son a small part of the kingdom. But the rest will be given to another."

Rebellions and intrigues came up so that when Solomon died after reigning for forty years, his son, Rehoboam, lost the northern ten tribes. They seceded and were called the Kingdom of Israel. Only the land of the tribe of Judah, in which Jerusalem was located, remained and was called The Kingdom of Judah. And so, nine hundred and thirty years before the birth of Jesus, the tribes were divided because of their unfaithfulness, never to re-unite. But God remains faithful.

# 7

# Wickedness Burns Like Fire

## *The Kingdom Ends*

*By the rivers of Babylon, we sat mourning and weeping when we remembered Jerusalem. On the trees of that foreign land we hung our harps. There our captors asked us for the words of a song; our tormentors for a joyful song; "Sing of us a song of Jerusalem!" But how could we sing a song of the Lord in a foreign land?*

*Psalm 137*

**Division**
From the First and Second Books of Kings and the First and Second Books Chronicles

Jeroboam, the king of Israel was jealous that his people had to travel to Jerusalem in the rival Kingdom of Judah to make sacrifices to the Lord, so he built shrines and temples in his own land and appointed men who were not Levites to be priests. He had golden calves made and placed in the temples and so fostered heresy.

About fifty years later the capital of Israel was moved to the city of Samaria and shortly after that King Ahab married Jezebel, the daughter of the king of Sidon. Ahab and Jezebel established the worship of Baal, the god of the Canaanites and suppressed the worship of the Lord. Temples to Baal were set up in Samaria and around the Kingdom of

Israel. Ahab and Jezebel arrested and executed many of the prophets of the Lord.

One Prophet, named Elijah, managed to escape the terrors of Jezebel. He hid for a while and, when the time was right, he returned to face King Ahab who he met on the road.

"Is that you, you disturber of Israel?" said the king.

Elijah answered, "It is not I who disturb Israel but you and your family by forsaking the Lord and turning to Baal. I challenge you to assemble all four hundred and fifty prophets of Baal on Mount Carmel." This Ahab agreed to do.

So, the prophets of Baal and many of the people had assembled on Mount Carmel. Elijah spoke to the people. "How long will you sit on the fence between Baal and the Lord?" The people did not answer so Elijah said, "I am the only surviving prophet of the Lord and here there are four hundred and fifty prophets of Baal. Let us set up an altar of burnt offerings to the Lord and one to Baal." And they did. Then Elijah said to the prophets of Baal, "Now sacrifice a bull, cut it up, and place it on the wood of the altar to Baal, but do not light the fire. I will do the same and place my offering on the wood of the altar to the Lord, but I will not light the fire. Let us see whose God answers with fire!"

The prophets of Baal set up their offering and began to pray for fire, but nothing happened. They prayed louder saying "Answer us Baal!" They danced around the altar and cut themselves with knives. But still, nothing happened. Elijah taunted them saying "Maybe you should pray louder, perhaps Baal is asleep." So, they prayed louder and went into trances and cut themselves more. But nothing happened.

Then Elijah had the people gather twelve large stones, one for each of the tribes of Israel. He set them up as an altar and had wood piled on. He sacrificed a bull and placed its pieces on the altar. "Fill four large jars with water and pour it over the sacrifice and the wood." This was done. "Again!" he said, and it was done. "A third time!" he said, and it was done, and the whole altar; wood and stones, was dripping with water. Then Elijah stood back. "Lord God of Abraham, Isaac, and Jacob," he said loudly, "I have done as you have commanded. Answer me now so these people may come back to their senses and know that you are God." A fire came down from the sky and burned up the offering and the wood and even burned up the stones and the dirt around.

The people fell on their faces saying, "The Lord is God, the Lord is God!" At Elijah's command they seized the prophets of Baal, not letting one escape, and executed them. Jezebel was thrown out of a high window of the palace by her own servants. Her body was left on the ground and became food for dogs.

## Prophets
From the Books of Isaiah, Jeremiah, and Micah

For a while, the people returned to the Lord, but it was not to last. Later generations in Israel and in Judah slipped back into the worship of Baal and of false gods. Corruption took hold in both kingdoms and justice became rare.

In time the Lord raised up another prophet, Isaiah, who received a calling from the Lord while in the temple at Jerusalem. At this time, the Hebrews were beset by enemies and many people, kings, and commoners, in both Judah and Israel had turned from the Lord. Isaiah was an adviser to King Ahaz of Judah, but the king did not take Isaiah's advice. Isaiah, inspired by God, issued a dire warning to the kingdoms of Israel and Judah...

"Hear, oh sky and listen, oh earth, for the Lord speaks: 'Sons have I raised and cherished, but they have abandoned me. An ox or an ass knows its master, but Israel does not know. Oh, sinful nation, evil race, corrupt children. What do I care for your sacrifices? I have had enough of them. I find no pleasure in the blood of calves and lambs. Make no more worthless offerings to me. When you pray, I will not listen.

"There is blood on your hands. Wash yourselves clean. Stop doing evil and learn to do good. Seek justice. Though your sins are red as blood they can be made white as snow. If you return to me, you shall enjoy the fruits of the land. If you resist me the sword shall come to you.'

"Jerusalem is crumbling," Isaiah said. "Judah is falling, for their evil speech and deeds are a provocation to the Lord. Their sin is like Sodom and they hide it not! Your men will fall by the sword and your champions die in war. Her gates will mourn, and the city be deserted.

"In Israel and Samaria wickedness burns like fire. You deprive the needy of justice; making widows your plunder and orphans you prey. What will you do on the day of judgement? The anger of the Lord seethes and his hand is stretched out toward you. He will give a sign to a far-off nation and they will come upon you. They will neither stumble nor rest. Their arrows are sharp, their horses' hooves are like flint, and their chariots like cyclones. They will growl like lions, seizing their prey and carrying it off and no one will rescue it. In those days, every place where there used to be rich vineyards shall be turned into briars and thorns.

"Who cups the seas in his hands? Who measures the sky with is fingers? Who knows the measure of the dust of the earth and the weight of the mountains? Do you not know, or have you not heard that the Lord is the eternal god, the creator of the ends of the earth? He does not grow tired. His knowledge is boundless. He gives strength to the weak and vigor to the weary. Those who hope in the Lord will be strengthened. They will soar as on eagles' wings. They will run and not grow weary, will walk and not be tired.

"Be silent then, Israel, and wait on the words of God; 'I, the Lord, am the first and the last of all things. You Israel are a maggot. You Judah, a worm. But I have chosen you; descendants of my friend Abraham. Be not afraid for I am with you. Be not dismayed, I am your God. In time I will strengthen you and help you and hold you in my right hand. All those who have opposed and oppressed you will perish and come to nothing. The land that was deserted and barren will bloom again. Waters will flow, trees and orchards will grow again so that all may see and know that the Lord, the Holy One of Israel, has done so.'

Isaiah wrote of the coming of a savior, saying, "A voice cries out in the wilderness 'Straighten and repair the roads for the coming of our God!' Then the glory of our God shall be revealed to all nations. Here comes your God. Like a shepherd he feeds his flock and gathers the lambs in is arms. The virgin shall be with child and bear a son, and shall call him

79

Emmanuel, that is 'God Among Us.' This shoot shall sprout from the stem of Jesse, David's father, and from his roots a descendant will rise up and the spirit of the Lord will rest upon him. And he shall be a sign to the nations, and they shall seek him out to follow him. In those times the people who had walked in darkness will see a great light. For a child is born to us, a son is given to us and on his shoulder dominion rests. He is called Wonderful counselor, God-Hero, Eternal Father, Price of Peace. His dominion is vast and forever in peace.

"The Lords says, 'Here is my servant, my chosen one with whom I am well pleased. He shall bring justice to the nations. Not shouting or speaking out. He shall not break a bruised reed nor quench a smoldering wick until he establishes justice on the Earth. The old things have come to pass, the new things I now tell you. Before they even happen, I announce them to you. My servant shall prosper and be raised up to the amazement of many since his appearance is so marred. Kings will be speechless and those who had not known will see.

Those who have not heard will ponder and say 'Why would we believe it. He grew up like a sapling from the dry ground and in him was nothing stately nor was he attractive. He was avoided by men. A man of suffering; used to suffering. Yet it was our infirmities that he bore, our sufferings that he endured. We thought nothing of him, but he was pierced for our crimes; crushed for our sins. Upon him was the punishment that makes us whole, by his stripes we were healed. We had all wandered astray, but The Lord laid on him all our guilt. Though he was abused he remained silent, without complaint. Like a lamb to the slaughter he was taken away and who would have thought any more of him? When he was executed for the sins of his people, he was laid among the graves of sinners though he had done nothing wrong."

The Lord says, "Because of his suffering, my servant shall see the light of day. Through his suffering, he shall justify many by bearing their guilt. And he shall be counted among the great."

Isaiah's foretelling of the downfall of the two kingdoms, and of eventual redemption, and of the coming of a champion was recorded and heeded by some but ignored by many. They did not take him seriously; how could he foretell the future? And what kind of champion is crushed and executed? How could a champion die for the sins of others like a sacrificial lamb and yet rule a vast kingdom in power and glory?

The Lord sent another prophet to echo the warnings of Isaiah. His name was Micah. Micah wrote, "Hear this, leaders of the house of Jacob, lords of Israel! You who hate what is just and pervert what is right. You pass judgement for a bribe, your priests give decisions for a salary, your prophets prophesy for money. Because of you, Jerusalem shall be reduced to rubble and the temple mount shall be a mere forest ridge.

"But you Bethlehem, too small a town to be counted among the tribes of Judah, from you shall come forth one who is to rule in Israel; whose origin is of old, from ancient times. He shall stand like a shepherd over his flock with the power of God, with the name of God. And his flock shall remain, for his greatness shall reach to the ends of the earth and he shall be peace."

Some believed. They called the future champion The Anointed One, a title for kings and high priests. In Hebrew Anointed One is "Messiah;" in Greek it is "The Christ." Who would he be; he who is to be born of a virgin in the tiny village of Bethlehem, he who was to suffer and be pierced and die for the sins of others like a sacrificial lamb, but who was to stand with the infinite power of God in the eternal name of God? From these times the faithful of Israel waited and watched for the coming of the Messiah. Each generation hoped the Messiah would come in their time. But the destruction would come first, and the people would have to wait.

The fortunes of the Kingdom of Israel waxed and waned until, two hundred years after seceding from Judah, the kingdom was invaded by the powerful Assyrian army. Samaria fell, and the land was overrun just as the prophets had said. Most of the people, men, women, and children, died by the sword or of terrible hunger. The pitiful survivors were taken as slaves by the Assyrians and disbursed throughout their empire and foreigners moved into their homes and the Kingdom of Israel was no more.

The fortunes of the Kingdom of Judah waxed and waned. Good king followed bad king, and bad king followed good king. There were times of peace and of war. There were times of heresy and times of orthodoxy. For a while, the kingdom fell under the influence of Egypt and, for a while, under the influence of Assyria. The people became known as "Jews" for they were of Judah and the rest of Israel had been lost. Another power arose in the east, the Babylonian Empire. Their king, Nebuchadnezzar made war upon Zedekiah, the king of Judah. Babylonians overran the land. After a long and tragic siege, they took Jerusalem and destroyed it, tearing down its walls, and looting and burning the temple of God. Many of the people of Judah were put out of their misery with the fires and swords of the Babylonians. Zedekiah and seventy thousand people were deported to Babylon as slaves. So, three hundred and fifty years after the death of Solomon, Judah became a Babylonian province and Jerusalem was an abandoned pile of rubble. The temple was but charred stone and there was no place for the people to make sacrifices to The Lord.

## Daniel
From the Book of Daniel

When Nebuchadnezzar had settled the Jewish slaves around his empire, he ordered that the most gifted young men be brought to the palace and taught Babylonian ways, so they could serve the king. Among them were four young men named Daniel, Shadrach, Meshach, and Abednego. Daniel especially found favor with Nebuchadnezzar because he could interpret dreams. When the king promoted Daniel, Daniel saw to it that Shadrach, Meshach, and Abednego were also promoted.

Nebuchadnezzar had a giant golden statue made and set up on the plain near Babylon. He decreed that all his governors and administrators come to the statue and bow down and worship it and if anyone refused, they would be tossed into a white-hot furnace. No good Jew would worship the statue of a false god, so when Shadrach, Meshach, and Abednego were brought before the statue they refused to bow down.

When Nebuchadnezzar was told of this, he had the three brought before him. "Is it true," he said, "that you will not serve my God or bow before the statue I made? I will give you another chance to bow down before the statue. If you do not, you will be cast into a white-hot furnace and what god can save you then?"

They answered him, "We make no defense. If our God will not save us, we will still not worship your god or bow down to a statue."

Nebuchadnezzar became enraged. He ordered the furnace heated to seven times its usual heat. Some of his strongest men tied up Shadrach, Meshach, and Abednego and threw them, fully clothed, into the furnace which was so hot that its flames consumed the men who had thrown them in. But soon, the king and his men could see the Jews standing inside the furnace among the searing flames and they could hear Abednego singing a song of praise to God.

The king's men continued to stoke the flames; throwing in sulfur, pitch, and bundles of wood. The flames rose nearly a hundred feet above the furnace and spread out, burning the men nearby. But an angel of The Lord was in the furnace, protecting the men from the flames as if a cool breeze was flowing through it. And all three men began singing songs to God.

Hearing them sing, and seeing them alive, the astonished king stood and said to his men, "Did we not throw three bound men into the fire? But now I see four unbound men walking in the fire, and one looks like the son of a god!" He went closer to the furnace entrance and shouted into it. "Servants of God, come out!"

When Shadrach, Meshach, and Abednego came out, the king and his men could see that they were unharmed. Not their clothes nor even a hair of the heads was singed. They did not even smell of smoke.

"Blessed be the God of Shadrach, Meshach, and Abednego who sent and angel to save them!" said the king. "I hereby proclaim that anyone who blasphemes the god of these men will be cut to pieces since no god can rescue like their god." And the king promoted Shadrach, Meshach, and Abednego.

Daniel had a dream. He saw strange and awful beasts. One of the beasts was like a leopard with four wings and four heads and it was given dominion. Then he saw the Ancient One sitting on a throne. He was gleaming white, and his throne was of fire and fire came out of the throne in streams. Thousands upon thousands and multitudes upon multitudes attended him. The beast was slain and thrown into the fire. Then, one like a son of man came on the clouds to the Ancient One and he was given dominion, glory, and kingship over all the nations of the earth. His dominion shall be forever, and his kingship shall never end. So, to Daniel, came a vision of the Messiah.

In time Nebuchadnezzar died. His heir, Belshazzar, became king of Babylon. King Belshazzar gave a great banquet for a thousand of his lords. Being drunk, he ordered that the sacred gold and silver vessels, which Nebuchadnezzar had taken from the temple in Jerusalem, be brought in so his lords and ladies could drink from them. They drank from the sacred vessels and praised their gods of metal, wood, and stone. Suddenly, in the light of a lamp stand, they saw a ghostly hand, writing with its fingers on the stone wall of the room.

The king's face went white and he shook to his core. He shouted for his magicians and astrologers to come and interpret the strange writing on the wall. Though they all came, none could read the writing, and the king and his lords were in turmoil.

News of the vision reached the queen and she came to Belshazzar and said, "O king, live forever! Do not be afraid for there is a man in your kingdom in whom is the spirit of God. When Nebuchadnezzar was king, this man was his chief advisor. His name is Daniel and he can interpret dreams and visions."

Daniel was sent for and when he came before the king, Belshazzar said, "Are you Daniel, the Jewish exile who was brought here by my father Nebuchadnezzar? I have heard that you can interpret dreams and possess great wisdom. My wise men cannot read the writing on this wall. If you can tell me what it means I will give you great riches."

"Keep your gifts, O king," said Daniel, "but I will read the writing for you and tell you what it means. Your father, Nebuchadnezzar was a mighty king who had the power of life and death over his people. Yet in his insolence he was humbled before The Lord. You have not humbled your heart but have rebelled against The Lord. He has seen His sacred vessels brought to you so you and your lords and ladies could drink from them in honor of your gods of metal, wood, and stone. But the God who holds your life in his hands, you did not honor. It is he who sent the hand to set the writing down.

"The words on the wall say 'Mene, Mene, Tekel, Peres.' This means: Mene; God has numbered your kingdom and it is at its end; Tekel, you have been weighed and found wanting; Peres, your kingdom has been divided and given to the Medes and the Persians."

That very night Belshazzar was killed. A Persian army entered Babylon unopposed and it became a possession of theirs and their king was Cyrus the Mede.


Cyrus decreed that any Jew who wished could return and rebuild Jerusalem and the Temple and worship the Lord God. Many Jews returned but many stayed including Daniel who was now and old man and who had been made a high official by the Persians.

After some time, Darius became emperor. Daniel was a high governor, a favorite of Darius; so much so that Darius had planned to make Daniel leader over the entire empire. This distressed some of the other governors and officials, so they planned the downfall of Daniel. They appealed to the vanity of the Emperor and suggested he sign a decree that, for thirty days, no one was to make a petition or plea to god or man except to the Emperor or they would be cast into a den of hungry lions. They knew Daniel prayed three times a day at his open window facing in the direction of Jerusalem. Darius, not knowing of this Jewish custom, signed the decree.

Daniel's enemies waited outside his window and they caught him praying. They then went to Darius and said, "Did you not decree, Oh King, that, for thirty days, anyone who was to make a prayer or petition to anyone but you was to be cast into a den of lions?"

"I did," said Darius.

The officials said, "Daniel, the Jewish exile has been praying to his god in disobedience to your decree."

At this Darius was greatly distressed for he loved Daniel. He tried to find a way to save Daniel, but the officials reminded him that, under the law of the Medes and Persians, any royal decree was irrevocable. So, Darius had Daniel brought to the door of the lions' den.

"May your god, who you serve so well, save you," he said as Daniel was put into the lions' den. Darius had a stone placed over the opening and placed his seal over it. He went back to his palace for the night. He dismissed his entertainer and courtiers and sat alone, unable to eat or sleep.

Very early the next morning he hastened to the lion's den. He called out, "Oh Daniel, who serves his god so well. Has you god saved you from the lions?"

Daniel answered from inside the den, "Oh King, live forever! My god has sent an angel to close the mouths of the lions and I am unharmed."

Overjoyed, Darius ordered Daniel to be released. He then ordered that his accusers be put into the lion's den and the lions quickly killed them all. He issued a decree, made in every language, that everywhere, the Living God of Daniel should be revered. Daniel fared well and died and old and honored man.

## Waiting
## From the Second Book of Chronicles and the First and Second Books of Maccabees

Those Jews who returned to Jerusalem did so in great joy, as if they were dreaming. The old men and women among them saw the places of their youth. The young men and women worked to rebuild the city and the temple. Over the time of several years, the city and temple were rebuilt, and sacrifices were made again in the temple. There were the peace offerings, the sin offerings, the burnt offerings, and all the pilgrimages and sacrifices of old, as set down by Moses so many centuries earlier. So, the words God had spoken through Isiah had at last come true; "The land that was deserted and barren will bloom again. Waters will flow, trees and orchards will grow again so that all may see and know that the Lord, the Holy One of Israel, has done so."

But foreigners were still among them. They had settled in all the land of Samaria and even intermarried with some of the Jews. They kept their heretical practices and made sacrifices not in the Temple, but on hill tops as the pagans did. There was an uneasy peace in the land but there was peace.

Generations passed and then about three hundred and thirty years before the birth of the Messiah, Alexander the Macedonian made war against the Persians. He was unstoppable. His army, with their long spears, followed him across the length and breadth of the vast Persian Empire conquering everything. Jerusalem surrendered and the Jews, like the rest of the known world, found themselves subjects of Macedonians and Greeks. Many people found the Greek culture attractive and they adopted Greek customs and dress. In time many Greeks settled in the area, building cities and establishing trade. But most Jews refused to assimilate into the Greek culture. A Greek king arose who tried to force the Jews to accept everything Greek, even the pagan Greek religion. The Jews revolted and won their freedom after a long and bloody struggle. Once again Jerusalem was the capitol of a free kingdom. But it was not to last. A new power arose. Mighty Rome had arisen from the West. Roman legions devoured kingdoms one by one until all of Israel's neighbors fell to their irresistible power. At last, alone and powerless, the Jewish kingdom had no choice but to submit to Rome.

And the kingdom broke its covenant with God, but God remains faithful.

During these centuries of shifting fortunes, the faithful of Israel celebrated the Passover and other holy days. They made pilgrimages and offered sacrifices. Generation after generation waited and watched for the promised Messiah; the descendant of David who would do no harm and somehow suffer for the sins of others, but would also bring a final victory and a lasting peace and a new covenant with Israel and with the entire world. From time to time men would rise and claim to be the Messiah but each was found to be false. Still the people waited, year after year. Old men watched for signs and young men stood ready. Young women hoped. "Is it I?" they wondered, "Will the Lord choose me to be the mother of the Messiah; the champion of Israel, and the savior of the world?"

# BOOK II
## THE SON
## GOD, A MAN, AND THE WORLD

## Redemption

The action of regaining or gaining possession of something in exchange
for payment; or clearing a debt.

# 1

# And You Will Name Him Jesus

## *The Beginning*

*You are my son; I am your father. Ask, and it is yours. I will make the nations your inheritance, the ends of the earth your possessions. With an iron rod you will shepherd them.*

*Psalm 2*

## In the Beginning
From the Good News According to John

In the beginning was the Word, and the Word was with God, and the Word was God. He was in the beginning with God. All things came into being through him, and without him nothing came into being. What came through him was life, and this life was the light of the world. The light shines in the darkness, and the darkness cannot defeat it.

He was in the world and the world came into being through him, yet the world did not know him. He came to his own people, but they did not accept him. But to those who did accept him, to them he gave the right to become children of God, those who believed in his name. They were children not by blood, nor by human will, but by God.

And the Word became a man and lived among us, and we saw his glory, as of the only son of God, full of grace and truth.

For God so loved the world that he gave his only begotten son that whoever believes in him might not perish but will have eternal life. For God did not send his son into the world to condemn the world, but so the world might be saved through him.

## The Foretelling of the Coming of the Prophet
From the Good News According to Luke

In the days when Herod was King of Judea, there was a priest named Zechariah. His wife was a descendant of Aaron, and her name was Elizabeth. They were both good and blameless people, but they were old, and they had no children. Once, Zechariah was chosen by lot to enter the temple of the Lord to burn incense. While Zechariah was inside, an angel of the Lord appeared before him, standing next to the incense altar. Zechariah was terrified.

"Do not be afraid, Zechariah," said the angel. "God has heard your prayers. Your wife will give birth to a son and you shall name him John, and he will bring great joy and happiness for he will be great in the sight of the Lord. He will be filled with the Holy Spirit, even in his mother's womb. He will go ahead of the Lord in spirit and power to turn the hearts of fathers toward their children, the disobedient to righteousness, and make people fit to receive the Lord."

"But how can I believe this," asked Zechariah, "for my wife and I are both old?"

"I am Gabriel, one who stands before God," answered the angel. "I was sent to proclaim these things to you. But since you did not believe me you will be unable to speak until the things I have said come to be."

Meanwhile the people outside wondered why he was taking so long in the temple. When he came out, he could not speak but tried to communicate through gestures and the people could tell he had seen a vision. When his turn for service in the Temple was over, he went home and his wife, Elizabeth, conceived. After becoming pregnant she went into seclusion praising and thanking God that, at last, she would be a mother.

# Foretelling of the Coming of the Messiah
From the Good News According to Luke and Matthew

In the sixth month of Elizabeth's pregnancy, the angel Gabriel was sent to a small town called Nazareth in the province of Galilee, to a virgin who was engaged to a man named Joseph, and the virgin's name was Mary.

Gabriel came to her and said "I salute you, Full of Grace. The Lord is with you!"

Mary was afraid and wondered how she, a peasant, could be addressed in such a noble way.

"Do not be afraid," said Gabriel, "for God favors you. You will conceive in your womb and bear a son, and you will name him Jesus. He will be great and will be called the Son of God, and the Lord will give him the throne of David, his ancestor, and he will rule forever over the house of Jacob, and his kingdom will have no end."

"But how can this happen," asked Mary, "since I am a virgin?"

Gabriel said, "The Spirit of God will come over you and the power of the Lord will overshadow you. Therefore, the child to be born to you will be called the Son of God.

"Elizabeth, you relative, has also conceived in her old age. And this is her sixth month of pregnancy because nothing is impossible for God."

"I am the handmaid of the Lord," said Mary, "May it be done to me as you have said." Then the angel left her.

When Joseph, Mary's fiancé, found out that Mary was with child, and knowing that it was not his, he decided to break off the engagement quietly and not cause any trouble for Mary and her family. But before he could do so, an angel came to him in a dream and said to him "Joseph, descendant of David, do not be afraid to take Mary as your wife for it is through the power of God that she has conceived a child. She will give birth to a son and you shall name him Jesus because he will save the people from their sins." Jesus means "I AM saves." All this was done to fulfill the prophesy of Isaiah; "The virgin shall be with child and bear a son, and shall call him Emmanuel, that is 'God Among Us.'"

When Joseph awoke, he did as the angel commanded and took Mary into his house, but he had no marital relations with her.

During those days Mary traveled to the hill country of Judea, to the house of Zechariah and her relative, Elizabeth.

When Elizabeth heard Mary's greeting, the child in her womb leapt, and Elizabeth, filled with the Holy Spirit, shouted "You are most blessed among women and most blessed is the fruit of your womb! And how can it be that the mother of my Lord should come visit me? The moment I heard your voice the child in my womb leapt for joy. Blessed are you who believed that the word of the Lord that was spoken to you would come true!"

And Mary said, "My soul proclaims the great glory of the Lord and my spirit rejoices in God, my savior. For He has looked upon my lowliness and from now on all generations will call me blessed. The Mighty One has done great things for me and His very name is holy! He shows mercy from age to age to all who trust him. With his mighty arm he has scattered the arrogant. He has cast down rulers from their thrones and lifted up the lowly. He has filled the hungry with good things and the rich he has sent away empty. He has helped his servant, Israel, remembering his mercy and the promises he made to our ancestors, to Abraham, and his descendants forever."

Mary stayed with Elizabeth for three months and then returned to Nazareth.

## The Birth of John the Baptist
From the Good News According to Luke

When Elizabeth's time came, she gave birth to a son. Elizabeth's neighbors and family celebrated with her that she had a child. When the boy was eight days old, they joined with Elizabeth and Zechariah for the celebration of his circumcision. They were going to name him Zechariah, after his father but Elizabeth said no, that he should be named John. They said that no one in their family was named John. So, they asked Zechariah.

Zechariah took a tablet and wrote upon it, "His name is John."

Then immediately his voice returned and, to the amazement of all, he began to speak.

Filled with the Holy Spirit, Zechariah said, "Blessed be the Lord, the god of Israel, for he has brought our redemption as he promised through his prophets.

"And you, my son, will be called the Prophet of The Most High for you will go ahead of the Lord to prepare his way. You will give the people knowledge of their salvation through the forgiveness of their sins, thanks to the tender mercy of God. The One From On High will come to us to shine light on those who live in darkness and to guide our feet onto the path of peace."

The people were amazed at what had been done and said, and word spread of the child John, and people wondered what the child would become since the hand of the Lord was on him.

## The Birth of the Messiah
From the Good News According to Luke and Matthew

In those days Caesar Augustus issued a decree that everyone within the Roman Empire be enrolled in a census. Therefore, Joseph took Mary and traveled from Nazareth in Galilee to Bethlehem in Judea because Bethlehem was the hometown of King David and, as such, it was the town of Joseph's family, and the town where he had to register. It was a journey of about a week. There were many people in Bethlehem and when Joseph arrived, there was no room in the inn for him and Mary. He found a stable and made it as clean and comfortable as he could, and they stayed there. While they were there Mary's time came and she gave birth to her son. She wrapped him in swaddling clothes, which are cloths that are snuggly wrapped around the child so as to feel like the womb, and they laid him in a feeding trough.

There were shepherds out in the fields that night, keeping watch over their flocks. Suddenly an angel of the Lord appeared before them and the glory of God shone around them and they were terrified.

"Do not be afraid," said the angel, "for I bring you news of great joy for all the people. For tonight, in the city of David, a savior has been born for you who is Messiah and Lord. This will be a sign for you; you will find the infant wrapped in swaddling clothes and lying in a feeding trough. Suddenly there appeared a great crowd of heavenly beings praising God and singing, "Glory to God in the highest and peace to his people on earth."

When the angels had gone, the shepherds left their flocks and ran to Bethlehem where they found Mary and Joseph and the baby, just as the angel had said. They told them, and the others nearby, of what the angel had proclaimed, and all who heard were amazed. Then the shepherds returned to their flocks praising God for all they had seen, and Mary kept all these things in her heart.

When the child was eight days old, he was circumcised and given the name Jesus as the angel had said. Several days later his parents took him to the temple in Jerusalem, which was only a few miles from Bethlehem, to dedicate him to the Lord and redeem him with the sacrifice of two pigeons according to the Law of Moses, since Jesus was a firstborn son. There was a man in Jerusalem named Simeon. He was a holy man who awaited the redemption of Israel, and the Spirit of God was with him. It was revealed to him that he would not die until he saw the awaited Messiah. Inspired by the Spirit, he came to the temple and when he saw Jesus and his parents, he took the child in his arms and said, "Now Lord, you may let your servant go in peace for my eyes have seen your salvation; a light of revelation to the Gentiles and a glory for your people Israel." Mary and Joseph were amazed at this. Simeon blessed them, and he said to Mary, "This child is destined for the fall and rise of many in Israel and to be a contradiction to many, and your own heart will be pierced, so the thoughts of many hearts will be revealed."

There was also a prophetess named Anna who lived in the temple. She came up to them and gave thanks to God and she spoke about Jesus to all who were awaiting the redemption of Jerusalem.

Meanwhile, wise men from the east came to Jerusalem saying "We seek the newborn King of the Jews. We saw his star at its rising and have come to honor him."

The city was buzzing with the news of the wise men and it came to the ears of Herod. Herod was the King of Judea but in truth he was a puppet of Caesar, for Judea was subject to Rome. Herod, a cruel and faithless man, saw the announcement of a new king of the Jews as a threat to his dynasty. He summoned his chief priests and scribes, those who best knew the writings of the prophets, and asked them where the Messiah was to be born.

They said, "In Bethlehem of Judea for it is written, 'And you Bethlehem of Judea, are not at all among the least of the rulers of Judah; for from you shall come a ruler who will shepherd my people Israel.'"

Then Herod called the wise men to him and said, "Go to Bethlehem and find the child. When you have found him, come and tell me where he is so that I too may go and honor him." In reality, he wanted to find the child to kill him.

The wise men set out for Bethlehem and the star which they had seen went ahead of them until it settled on the place where the child was. Overjoyed by the presence of the star, they entered the place and found the child and his mother, Mary. They bowed down before him as to a king and they opened their treasure chests and gave him gifts of gold, frankincense, and myrrh. Gold; the traditional gift for a king, frankincense; a precious resin burned by priests to worship God, myrrh, an expensive spice used in funerary rites. Later, they were warned in a dream not to return to Herod, so they went home by another route.

When the wise men had left, an angel came to Joseph in a dream and said, "Rise and take the child and his mother to Egypt and stay there until I tell you. Herod is going to search for the child to kill him." Joseph did as he was told.

When Herod realized that the wise men were not coming back, he became furious. He ordered the death of every boy in and around Bethlehem who was two years old or younger. Then was fulfilled the words of the prophet Jeremiah; "A sound was heard in far off Ramah, crying and loud lamentation; Rachel weeping for her children, and she could not be comforted, for they were no more."

Sometime later Herod died, and the angel came to Joseph in a dream and told him to return to the land of Israel for those who sought the child's life are dead. Joseph took his family out of Egypt and they settled in Nazareth.

## The Finding in the Temple
From the Good News According to Luke

When Jesus was twelve years old, Joseph took Mary and Jesus to Jerusalem for Passover. This was the annual festival, held in the spring, to commemorate the time when Moses instructed the Israelites to sacrifice a lamb and spread its blood on their doors so that death would pass over those houses and fall upon the Egyptians, taking the firstborn of all of them even of their animals. Every year, all of Israel celebrated the Passover by traveling to Jerusalem for the weeklong festival that ended in the sacrifices of thousands of lambs and animals in the temple and its courtyards. The city of several thousand, for that week, became a city of several hundred thousand, even a million or more. Every house had its guests, every square had its tents, and every street had its cots. A sea of tents sprang up around the city and every town for a day's walk was filled with pilgrims.

After the days of the Passover celebration, Joseph and Mary started for home. They traveled for a full day thinking that Jesus was in their caravan. When they realized he had not been around, they searched for him among their friends and relatives in the caravan, but he was not there. They returned to Jerusalem and searched for him for three days in the great city. After three days they found him in the temple sitting with a group of teachers, asking questions, and all the teachers were amazed at his understanding.

His mother rushed to him and said, "Son, how could you do this to us? Your father and I have been worried sick! We were looking all over the city for you."

"Why were you looking all over the city for me?" he said. "Didn't you know that I would be in my Father's house?"

They did not understand what he meant. He went with them back to Nazareth and was obedient to them, and his mother kept all these things in her heart.

## The Ministry of John the Baptist
From the Good News According to Mathew, Luke, and John

In the fifteenth year of the rule of Tiberius Caesar, when Pontius Pilot was governor of Judea and Herod, the son Herod the baby killer, was prince over Galilee, the Holy Spirit came to John, the son of Zechariah, who was now about thirty years old, and he went around the region of the Jordan River calling on people to change their way because the time of the Messiah was at hand. He went about in the desert, wearing a rough camel hair tunic and a leather belt and for his food he ate locusts and wild honey. People came to him from all around Judea and beyond and he baptized them in the Jordan River. Baptism, or ritual washing, was required by the Law, and was done by the priests and people when they came to make prayers and sacrifices. The baptism of John was a sign of forgiveness and a new beginning.

When they asked him who he was, he said, "I am a voice crying out in the wilderness. 'Straighten and repair the roads for the coming of our God,'" as is written in the book of the prophet Isaiah.

One day he saw a group of Pharisees and a group of Sadducees approaching. The Pharisees were scribes and scholars who were very well educated in the Law of Moses. They were legalistic and added laws that were difficult to keep because, for them, the letter of the law was more important than the spirit of the law. The Sadducees were the priestly elite in Jerusalem who did not recognize the authority of the prophets but believed only in the books of Moses. Both groups had grown very powerful and many among them were very corrupt.

"You brood of vipers!" said John as they approached. "Who warned you to flee from the coming wrath? Produce good fruit if you really do want forgiveness. And do not claim salvation just because you are descendants of Abraham, for I'm telling you that God can raise up children to Abraham from these stones. Even now the ax is resting on the tree trunk. Any tree that does not bear good fruit will be cut down and thrown into the fire."

The people asked him what they should do, and he said, "Whoever has two cloaks should give one to someone who has none and whoever has enough food should do the same."

Tax collectors asked him what they should do, and he said, 'Stop collecting more than what is fair." Soldiers asked him what they should do, and he said, "Do not abuse your authority for personal gain, and be satisfied with your wages."

People began to wonder if he was the long-awaited Messiah, and he said, "I am not the Messiah. I am baptizing you with water but one mightier than I is coming, and he will baptize you with the Holy Spirit and with fire. I am not worthy to untie his sandals. He will come to gather the wheat into his barn, but the chaff will be burned with unquenchable fire."

John was not afraid to criticize Herod, the prince. This younger Herod was a prince, not a king like his father, for the Romans had taken that title away. The younger Herod was a cruel and inept ruler. He had divorced his first wife to marry Herodias who was his sister-in-law who had divorced Herod's brother to marry Herod.

One day, while John was baptizing in the Jordan River, Jesus arrived. When John saw him coming, he shouted to the crowd, "Look and see the Lamb of God who takes away the sin of the world! It is of him that I said, 'One is coming after me who is greater than me because he existed before me.'" This he said even though he was six months older than Jesus.

When John understood that Jesus had come to be baptized, he said, "I need to be baptized by you and yet you come to me?"

Jesus said, "Allow it for now, for in this way we will fulfill all righteousness." So, John baptized Jesus.

When Jesus stepped out of the river the heavens opened and the Holy Spirit of God came down like a dove and rested on him. And a voice said, "This is my beloved son with whom I am well pleased."

John said, "Now I have seen and testified that he is the Son of God." And John told his own followers to follow Jesus.

## The Temptation of Jesus
From the Good News According to Matthew

From the banks of the Jordan, Jesus went alone into the desert where he fasted and prayed in contemplation of his mission to come. After he was there for forty days, Satan came to him and, knowing how hungry Jesus was, he said, "If you are the Son of God command these stones to become loaves of bread."

Jesus replied, "It is written that one does not live by bread alone, but by every word that comes from the mouth of God."

Then the Devil took him and placed him on a high point on the temple in Jerusalem. He said, "If you are the Son of God, jump. For it is written that God will command his angels to hold you up, so you don't hit your foot against a stone."

Jesus said, "It is also written that you shall not test the Lord your God."

Then Satan took him to a very high mountain and showed him all the kingdoms of the Earth and all their splendor. He said, "All these kingdoms I will give to you if you simply bow down and worship me."

Jesus said, "Go away Enemy. For it is written that you shall worship God and God alone!"

At that Satan left him and angels came to minister to him.

# 2

# He Will Increase

*The First Year*

*Whoever clings to me, I will deliver. Whoever knows my name, I will raise up. All who call upon me will be answered, I will be with them in their distress, I will save them and honor them. I will show them my saving power.*

*Psalm 91*

**The Wedding at Cana**
From the Good News According to John

Jesus returned to Galilee and began preaching. People started following him, believing that he might be the Messiah. Among them were Phillip and Nathaniel as well as Andrew and his brother Simon; they were fishermen from the town of Bethsaida on the shores of the Sea of Galilee.

There was a wedding in the town of Cana, which was not far from Nazareth. Jesus was there with his mother and some of his followers. After a while, the wine began to run out. Jesus' mother said to him, "They have no more wine."

"Dear Woman," replied Jesus, "how will this affect you and I, for my death is still some time away?"

Mary, as she always did, pondered what her son had said, and she understood that, if he were to perform a miracle that day, it would be the end of their lives together and, that from that moment on, he would belong to the world. Even so, she went to the waiters and said, "Do whatever he tells you."

There were six large jars for washing before the meal, as was customary. They were about twenty-five gallons each. "Fill them with water," Jesus said. So, they filled them to the brim. Jesus said, "Now draw a cup out of one of the jars and take it to the headwaiter." They did so.

The headwaiter tasted it and found it to be wine, though he did not know where it came from. He went to the groom and said, "Everybody serves good wine first. Then, after people have been drinking, they serve the inferior wine. But you have saved the best wine for last."

This was the first of Jesus' miracles where he revealed his glory, and his followers began to really believe in him. He began to go from town to town and teach in their synagogues and he would move the hearts of the people. The number of his followers increased and many, including his mother, would travel with him and some would give money to finance the ministry.

## Passover in Jerusalem
From the Good News According to John

Not long after the wedding, Jesus and his followers went to Jerusalem for Passover as was customary. Upon entering the temple courtyard, which was supposed to be a sacred place, he saw merchants selling sheep and doves for sacrifice. He also saw that money changers had set up tables to exchange Roman money for temple money, since Roman money was not to be used in the temple. These people were doing their business inside the sacred spaces and were charging very high prices for the pilgrims who had no choice but to pay. He made a whip out of cords and drove the merchants out along with their animals, and he turned over the tables of the money changers. To the merchants selling animals he said, "Take these out of here and stop using my Father's house for a marketplace!"

The Jews in charge said to him, "What gives you the right to do this? What sign can you give us for your authority?"

Jesus said, "Destroy this temple and in three days I will raise it up." The temple at that time had been recently renovated under Herod, and it was huge.

The Jews said, "It took forty-six years to build this temple and you can raise it up in three days?" They did not understand that he was foretelling his own death and resurrection.

While in Jerusalem, Jesus preached and performed miracles and many people came to believe in him, and his followers baptized many.

One evening, while Jesus was still in Jerusalem, a leader among the Jews, a Pharisee named Nicodemus, came to him to talk. "Teacher," he said, "we know you are from God because of the miracles we have seen."

Jesus said, "No one can see God unless he is born from above."

"How can a man, once born, be born again?" asked Nicodemus.

Jesus said, "It is true. No one can enter the kingdom of God without being born of water and the Holy Spirit."

"How can this be?" said Nicodemus.

Jesus said, "You are a teacher of Israel and yet you don't understand me. I talk of what we know but you people do not accept my testimony. If you do not believe what I say about earthly things how will you believe if I tell you of heavenly things?"

After these things happened, the Pharisees and scribes of Jerusalem began to keep a close eye on Jesus.

## The Last Testimony of John
From the Good News According to John

Jesus and his followers went about Judea preaching and baptizing. Some people went to John the Baptist to tell him that Jesus' followers were now baptizing more people than he was.

John said, "No one can receive anything unless it is given from heaven. You already know that I am not the Messiah, but I come before the Messiah. The groom has the bride, but the best man is still happy for the groom. In the same way, my joy for Jesus is complete. He will increase, and I will decrease. The one who God sent speaks the words of God. The Father loves the Son and has given everything over to him. Whoever loves the Son has eternal life. Whoever disobeys the Son will not have eternal life."

Not long after this, Herod had John arrested and thrown into prison because of his criticism of Herod's marriage to his sister-in-law. Then Jesus and his followers returned to Galilee.

## The Woman at the Well
From the Good News According to John

To get from Judea to Galilee, Jesus had to pass through Samaria. The people of Samaria were of mixed blood; descendants of the people of the northern kingdom of Israel, which fell into heresy after splitting with Jerusalem, and of foreigners who settled there after Israel fell to the Assyrians. They believed in the One God and in the coming of the Messiah, but some pagan ideas filtered into their thinking, and they did not hold the temple in Jerusalem as a holy place. Because of this, the Jews considered them to be traitors and polluters of the faith and they had nothing to do with them.

In Samaria, Jesus came to a town called Sychar near a well that had been dug by Jacob many centuries earlier. He had sent his followers into the town to buy food while he stayed and waited by the well. A Samaritan woman came up to draw water from the well.

"Give me a drink," said Jesus to the woman.

The woman was surprised. "How can you, a Jew, ask me, a Samaritan, for water?"

Jesus said, "If you knew who had asked you for water, you would have asked him, and he would have given you living water."

"Sir," she said, "you don't even have a bucket and the well is deep. Are you greater than our father Jacob who built this well and drank from it himself?"

Jesus said, "Whoever drinks this water will be thirsty again but whoever drinks the water I will offer will never thirst, for the water I will give will be like a spring welling up and giving eternal life."

She said, "Sir, give me some of this water so that I may never be thirsty and won't have to come to draw water anymore."

"Go get your husband and come back," said Jesus.

"Sir," she said, "I have no husband."

Jesus answered, "You speak the truth, for you have had five husbands, and the man you are with now is not your husband."

"Sir," she said, "you must be a prophet! But your people worship in Jerusalem while mine worship God on our mountain."

Jesus said, "Your people believe what you do not understand while my people believe what they do understand, for salvation is from the Jews. But believe me, woman, the hour is coming when you will not worship God on your mountain or in Jerusalem. The hour is coming, and is in fact here, when true believers will worship the Father in Spirit and in truth. The Father seeks such people to worship him for the Father is Spirit and those who worship must worship in Spirit and truth."

The woman said, "I know the Messiah will come and he will explain all these things to us."

"I am he," said Jesus. "You are speaking with him."

The woman returned to the town and said, "Come and meet a man who has told me everything I have done. Could he be the Messiah?"

The people of the town went out to meet Jesus. After talking with him a while they invited him to stay with them which he did for two days. After he had left, they said to the woman, "We no longer believe because of what you told us, for we have heard his words ourselves, and we know that this is truly the savior of the entire world." And, after that, many Samaritans came to believe.

## Miracles in Galilee
From the Good News According to Luke and John

Jesus went to Nazareth, where he had grown up, and went to the synagogue for the Sabbath services. By then he had gained the title of "teacher" because of his preaching. At the proper time in the service, he was given a scroll containing the writings of Isaiah. He opened it to a certain passage about the Messiah and began to read, "The Spirit of the Lord is upon me for he has anointed me to bring good news to the poor, to proclaim liberty to captives, and recovery of sight to the blind; to free the oppressed, and to proclaim an age acceptable to the Lord."

When he had finished, he handed the scroll to the attendant and sat down. All eyes were on him. Then he said, "Today this prophesy is fulfilled in your hearing."

The men began to murmur among themselves saying, "Isn't this the carpenter, the son of Joseph the carpenter? We know him, we know his mother and his family." They were wondering how this man they saw grow up could have the nerve to proclaim himself to be the Messiah.

Jesus said, "No prophet is accepted in his own place. In the days of Elijah, there were many widows in need in Israel, but he went to Sidon to aid a foreign woman. When the prophet Elisha was alive there were many lepers in Israel, but he cured a Syrian man."

The men became angry because now, not only was this man proclaiming himself to be the sacred Messiah, but now he was saying that foreigners could be favored instead of Israelites, God's own people! To them this was blasphemy which at that time was punishable by death. They became a mob and they drove him out of the synagogue to the edge of the cliff on which Nazareth was built for they intended to throw him off. But he passed through the middle of them unharmed and left Nazareth.

Then he went to Cana. There was a royal official who lived in Capernaum, which was a two- or three-day's walk from Cana. When he heard that Jesus was in Cana, he went to ask Jesus to come with him to Capernaum to heal his son who was near death. "Please come before my child dies," he said.

Jesus said, "You may go; your son shall live."

The official believed Jesus and went back along the road down to Capernaum. During his return he met his slaves on the road who were coming to see him to tell him that the boy was better.

"When did this happen?" he said.

They answered, "The fever left him yesterday at about one in the afternoon."

The official realized that that was just the time when Jesus had told him "Your son will live." He and his whole household came to believe.

Then Jesus and his followers went to Capernaum which was a large town on the banks of the Sea of Galilee, which was a lake about twelve miles in diameter. He preached there for a while and cured many people of their illnesses including the mother-in-law of Simon, the son of Jonah.

At dawn he went out of Capernaum to a quiet place on the shore, but many people had come to hear and see him, and they found him and asked him to return to town. He explained that he was preparing to go to other towns, but they were anxious to be with him, and they hemmed him in against the shore. There were two boats on shore with fishermen who were washing their nets after being out fishing the night before. One of the boats belonged to Simon, the son of Jonah and his brother, Andrew, and the other boat belonged to James and John, the sons of Zebedee. Jesus got into Simon's boat and asked him to put out from the shore which he did. Then Jesus sat in the boat and preached to the crowd on the shore.

When he was finished teaching, he said to Simon, "Go out into deep water and cast out your nets for a catch."

Simon answered, "Master, we have been fishing all night and have caught nothing, but, since you say so, I will do it." When they had done this, they caught so many fish that they could not bring them in, and the nets were about to tear. They signaled to the other boat to come help them. When they had pulled in the catch, it was so big that both boats were full to the point of sinking.

At this Simon fell to his knees before Jesus and said, "Leave me Lord, for I am a sinner."

"Do not be afraid," said Jesus. "Follow me, and I will make you fishers of men."

When they pulled into shore all four men left everything and followed Jesus.

One day Jesus was teaching at a house in Capernaum. The house was crowded with listeners. Some men brought a paralyzed man on a stretcher, but they could not get through the crowd. They went up to the roof of the house and removed some roof tiles and lowered the paralyzed man on the stretcher right down in front of Jesus.

When Jesus saw their faith, he said to the paralyzed man "Your sins are forgiven."

Now in the crowd were scribes and Pharisees from Galilee as well as some who had been sent from Jerusalem to keep an eye on Jesus. They began to whisper to themselves, "Who is this man who commits blasphemy? Only God can forgive sins."

Jesus said to them, "Why are you thinking evil? Which is easier; to say, 'your sins are forgiven' or to say, 'rise and walk'? But, so you may know that the Son of Man has authority to forgive sins," he told the paralyzed man, "Rise and pick up your stretcher and go home."

The man immediately got up, picked up what he had been lying on, and went home praising God. All who saw this were amazed and began to praise God. And word of this event spread far and wide.

# 3

# Follow Me

*The Second Year*

*Some went down to the sea to make their living on the water. They saw the wonders of The Lord. He spoke and roused a storm that tossed waves that rose up to the sky and sank down to the depths. Their skill was useless so, in their fear, they cried out to The Lord. He saved them from danger; hushed the storm and calmed the waves. Let them thank God for such kindness to mere mortals. Let them praise Him and give thanks.*

*Psalm 107*

## Another Passover in Jerusalem
From the Good News According to John

Jesus and his followers went to Jerusalem to celebrate their second Passover together. There were pools near the temple where people could wash, ritually cleansing, or baptizing themselves before entering the temple precincts. One of these pools was called Bethesda. From time to time water would well up in this pool from underground and some people would be cured by this welling up. Many sick, blind, and crippled people were there. One crippled man had been there for thirty-eight years.

When Jesus saw the man, he asked him, "Do you want to be well?"

The man said, "I have no one to assist me so when the water wells up, I take too long, and people always crowd in before me."

110

Jesus said to him, "Get up, pick up your mat, and walk."

And so, the man got up and picked up his mat and walked.

This was on a Sabbath day and it was forbidden to work on a Sabbath day. The Jewish leaders found out about this and, considering curing to be work, they confronted Jesus about it.

Jesus said to them, "My father is at work, so I am at work. A son does what he sees his father doing; for a father who loves his son shows him what he himself does. Whoever does not honor the son dishonors the father who sent him. Whoever hears my words and believes in the one who sent me will have eternal life for he has passed from death to life. Even now, the dead hear the voice of the Son of God and are brought to life. And the Son of God is given power to judge because he is also the Son of Man."

This is when Jesus revealed himself as Son of God and Son of Man. Others had called him the Son of God because of the wonders they had seen. But Jesus referred to himself as the Son of Man, recalling Daniel's dream when he saw "one like a son of man who came on the clouds to the Ancient One and he was given dominion, glory, and kingship over all the nations of the earth. His dominion shall be forever, and his kingship shall never end." Though they did not understand at this time that the Lamb of God who would be sacrificed had to be the Son of Man because of the guilt of man, but also the Son of God because of the mercy of God who alone had the power to redeem mankind.

Jesus went on to tell them, "John testified on my behalf and his testimony was true. You sent emissaries to him to hear his testimony and you were happy with it. But my testimony is greater than his. The works that the Father gave me to perform, these are my testimony. Moreover, the Father himself has testified on my behalf in the scriptures and through the prophets. You search the scriptures because you think the scriptures will save you, but they do not help you because you don't want to come to me for eternal life."

As Jesus left, he saw a tax collector named Matthew sitting at the customs post. Tax collectors were considered traitors by the Jews since they collected taxes for their Roman oppressors. They were also notorious for overcharging people and pocketing the difference.

Jesus said to him, "Follow me," and immediately Matthew got up and went with Jesus.

He had Jesus over to his house for a meal, and while Jesus and his followers were there, other tax collectors and sinners came and joined them.

The Pharisees who had been following Jesus saw this as an opportunity to trip him up. They said to Jesus's followers, "Why does your teacher eat with sinners and tax collectors?"

Jesus heard them and said, "Those who are well do not need a doctor, but the sick do. You should learn the meaning of the sacred writings that say, 'I desire mercy, not sacrifice.' I did not come to call the righteous, but the sinners." After that Matthew became one of Jesus' followers.

## The Calling of the Twelve
From the Good News According to Mark and Luke

After returning to Galilee, Jesus withdrew to the top of a mountain to pray. When he came down, he called his followers together and he chose twelve from among them to be sent out to preach and teach and work miracles as testimony to Jesus. In Greek, the word "apostle" means "one who is sent" and so these men became known as The Twelve Apostles, or, in English "The Twelve Who are Sent." They were Simon Son of Jonah, and his brother Andrew, James and John, the sons of Zebedee, Philip, Bartholomew, Matthew, Thomas, James the son of Alpheus, Thaddeus, Simon of Cana, and Judas Iscariot who would betray him. There were also many women who followed him from place to place and helped to support his ministry. They included Mary of Magdala who had been cured of seven demons, and Joanna, the wife of Herod's steward, Chuza.

## The Sermon on the Mount
From the Good News According to Matthew

Jesus went around Galilee, teaching in their synagogues, proclaiming the good news of the Kingdom of God, and curing their illnesses. His fame spread all over Galilee, Judea, Phoenicia, and Syria. Great crowds came to hear him, and they brought their sick, their lame, their lunatics, and the paralyzed and he cured them all.

One day Jesus went up a hillside and sat down and his followers came after him and he began to teach them saying, "Blessed are the poor in spirit, for theirs is the Kingdom of Heaven. Blessed are they who mourn, for they will be comforted. Blessed are the meek, for they will inherit the land. Blessed are those who hunger and thirst for righteousness, for they will be satisfied. Blessed are the merciful, for they will receive mercy. Blessed are the clean of heart, for they will see God. Blessed are the peacemakers, for they will be called children of God. Blessed are those who are persecuted for the sake of righteousness, for theirs is the Kingdom of Heaven. Blessed are you when they insult you and persecute you and utter all kind of evil falsely about you because of me. Rejoice and be glad, for your reward in Heaven will be great. So, too, they persecuted the prophets before you.

"You are the salt of the earth. But if salt loses its flavor, what can be seasoned with it? It is good for nothing but to be thrown out. You are the light of the world. A city set on a hill cannot be hidden. Nor do they light a lamp and hide it under a bushel basket. It is set on a lampstand where it gives light to everyone in the house. In the same way, your light must shine before others, that they may see the good that you do and glorify your heavenly Father.

"Do not think that I have come to abolish the law or the prophets. I have not come to abolish, but to fulfill. Truly, until heaven and earth pass away, not the smallest part of the smallest letter of the law shall pass until all things are fulfilled. Therefore, whoever breaks the least of the commandments and teaches others to do so, will be called the least in the Kingdom of Heaven. But whoever obeys and teaches the commandments will be called the greatest in the kingdom of Heaven. So, unless your righteousness surpasses that of the Scribes and Pharisees, you will not enter the Kingdom of Heaven.

"You have heard it said, 'You shall not kill; and whoever kills will be liable to judgment.' But I say to you, whoever is angry with his brother will be liable to judgment, and whoever insults his brother will be answerable, and whoever says 'you fool' will be liable to the flames. Therefore, if you bring a sacrifice to the altar and there remember that your brother has something against you, go and settle with your brother first, and then offer your sacrifice.

"You have heard it said, 'You shall not commit adultery.' But I say to you whoever looks at a woman with lust has already committed adultery in his heart. If your right eye causes you to sin, pluck it out and throw it away. It is better to enter the Kingdom of Heaven with one eye than to have your whole body cast into Hell. And if your right hand causes you to sin, cut it off and throw it away. It is better to enter the Kingdom of Heaven with one hand than to have your whole body thrown into Hell.

"You have heard it said, 'whoever divorces his wife must give her a bill of divorce.' But I say to you whoever divorces his wife of a lawful marriage causes her to commit adultery, and whoever marries a divorced woman commits adultery.

"Again, you have heard it said to your ancestors 'Do not make false oaths but make good what you swear to the Lord.' But I say to you do not swear at all; not by heaven for it is the throne of God, nor by the earth, for it is God's footstool. Let your 'yes' mean yes and your 'no' mean no. Anything else is from the Evil One.

"You have heard it said, 'An eye for an eye and a tooth for a tooth.' But I say to you, offer no resistance to one who does you evil. If someone slaps you on the cheek, turn the other cheek as well. If someone wants to take you to court over your tunic, give him your tunic and your cloak as well. If a soldier orders you to carry his gear for a mile, carry it for two miles. Give to one who asks, and do not ignore one who wants to borrow.

"You have heard it said, 'Love your neighbor and hate your enemy." But I say to you, love your enemies, and pray for your persecutors, so you may be children of God, for he makes his sun rise on the good and on the bad, and the rain to fall on the just and the unjust. If you love only those who love you, what will your reward be? Don't tax collectors do the same? And if you greet only your friends, what good is that? Don't pagans do the same? So be perfect just as your heavenly Father is perfect. But take care not to do good just so others may see you. Do not be like hypocrites who do good deeds so others may admire them. I tell you they have received their reward. But when you give, do not let your left hand know what your right hand is doing, so when you give in secret your heavenly Father, who sees in secret, will reward you.

"When you pray don't be like hypocrites who pray in public only so that they can be seen. They have already received their reward. But when you pray go to your room and pray in secret, and your heavenly Father, who sees in secret, will repay you. And do not pray like the pagans who babel on and on, trying to get the attention of their false gods. Your heavenly father knows what you need even before you ask.

"This is how you should pray: 'Our Father who is in Heaven, holy is your name. May your kingdom come, and may your will be done on earth as it is done in heaven. Give us today our daily bread; and forgive us our offences in the same way we forgive those who offend us; and do not let us fall to temptation but save us from the Evil One.'

"If you forgive others, your heavenly Father will forgive you. But if you do not forgive others, neither will your heavenly Father forgive you.

"When you fast, do not look sad like the hypocrites do so others may know they are fasting. They have already been paid. When you fast, wash and groom yourself so that no one may know you are fasting. So fast in private and your heavenly Father, who sees in private, will reward you.

"Do not store up for yourselves treasure on earth where moth and rust destroy, and thieves break in and steal. Rather, store up for yourselves treasure in heaven where neither moth nor rust destroy, nor thieves break in and steal. For, wherever your treasure is, so also your heart will be.

"No one can serve two masters. He will either hate one and love the other or be devoted to one and neglect the other. You cannot serve God and money. So, do not worry about your life; what you will eat or drink, or about your body; what you will wear. Is not life more than food and the body more than clothes? Look at the birds of the sky; they do not plant or harvest, they gather nothing into barns, yet your heavenly Father feeds them. Aren't you more important than they are? Can any of you by worrying add a single moment to your life? Why are you so concerned with clothes? Look how the wildflowers grow. They do not work or weave.

Yet I tell you that not even Solomon with all his wealth was clothed like one of them. If God so clothes the plants of the field which grow today and are burned tomorrow will he not provide so much more for you, oh you of little faith? So, do not worry and say, 'What shall we eat or what shall we wear?' Those are the things the pagans worry about. Your heavenly Father knows you need those things. But you should first seek the kingdom of God and his righteousness, and all those things will be given to you besides. Don't worry about tomorrow; tomorrow will take care of itself. Today has enough trouble of its own.

"Stop judging others so you will not be judged. For as you judge others, so will you be judged. Why do you notice the splinter in your brother's eye, but you don't notice the beam in your own eye? How can you say to your brother 'Let me help you remove that splinter,' when the beam is in your eye? Hypocrite! Remove the beam from your own eye first, then you will see clearly to remove the splinter from your brother's eye.

"Ask and it will be given to you. Seek and you will find. Knock and the door will be opened to you. Which of you would give his son a stone when he asked for a loaf of bread, or a snake when he asked for a fish? If you then, who are flawed, know how to give good things to your children, how much more will your heavenly Father give to those who ask?

"Do to others what you would have them do to you. This is the sum of the law and the prophets.

"Enter through the narrow gate; for the gate is wide and the road broad that leads to destruction, and those who take it are many. How narrow is the gate and the road that lead to life, and those who take it are few.

"Beware of false prophets who come to you in sheep's clothing but inside are hungry wolves. You do not pick grapes from thorn bushes or figs from thistles. Likewise, a good tree bears good fruit and a bad tree bears bad fruit. So, by their fruits you will know them.

"Not everyone who says to me 'Lord, Lord' will enter the Kingdom of Heaven, but only those who do the will of my Father in Heaven. Many will say to me on the Last Day 'Lord, Lord, didn't we prophesy in your name? Didn't we drive out demons in your name? Didn't we do mighty deeds in your name?' Then I will say to them solemnly 'Leave me you evil doers, I never knew you.'

"Whoever listens to my words and acts on them is like a wise man who built his house on rock. The rains came, the floods rose, and the wind blew and buffeted the house. But it held strong since it had been set firmly on rock. But whoever listens to my words and does not act on them is like a foolish man who built his house on sand. The rains came, the flood rose, and wind blew and buffeted the house. And it collapsed and was completely ruined."

## Jesus and the Centurion
From the Good News According to Matthew

Jesus returned to Capernaum. As he entered the city, a centurion approached him. A centurion was an officer of the occupying Roman army. The Jews avoided the Romans because they were their oppressors and were pagans.

"Lord," said the centurion, "my servant is lying sick at home. He cannot move and is in great pain."

"I will come see him," said Jesus.

The centurion answered, "Lord, I am not worthy that you should enter under my roof, but only say the word and my servant will be healed. For I, too, am a man of authority, with many men under my command. And if I say to one 'go' he goes, and another 'come' he comes. And if I tell my slave 'do this' he does it."

Jesus said to those gathered around, "I have not found such faith even among the men of Israel. I tell you, many foreigners will come from the east and from the west and will feast at the banquet in Heaven with Abraham, Isaac, and Jacob while the children of Israel will be driven out into the darkness where there will be wailing and grinding of teeth." Then he said to the centurion, "You may go. Since you have believed, it will be done." And at that very hour, his servant was healed.

## Raising of a widow's son
From the Good News According to Luke

Then Jesus went to a town in Galilee called Nain. A great crowd of people was following him. As he arrived at the gate, a funeral procession was coming out bearing the coffin. The dead man was the only son of a widow, and now his mother had no one to support her. When Jesus saw her among the mourners he was moved with pity.

"Don't cry," he said. Then he stepped forward and touched the coffin. He said, "Young man, get up."

Immediately the man sat up and began to speak and Jesus took him to his mother.

The crowd was seized with great fear and they began praising God. Some said, "A great prophet has come among us!" Others said, "God Himself has come among us!" And news of this event spread not only throughout all Judea but even throughout all the neighboring lands.

## Messengers from John the Baptist
From the Good News According to Luke

Followers of John the Baptist came to him in prison and told him about the man who was working wonders throughout Galilee and Judea. Being in prison, John could not see the man for himself, whether it was Jesus or another. So, he sent two messengers to speak with him.

When they found Jesus they said, "John the Baptist has sent us to you. We are to ask you if you are the one who is to come, or should we look for another?"

Before he answered them, he went among the crowd and cured many of their diseases and much of their pain. He cast out demons and cured some blind people. Then he said to them, "Go tell John what you have seen and heard; the blind regain sight, the lame walk, lepers are cured, the deaf hear, the dead are raised, and the poor hear the good news. And blessed is the one who accepts me."

After the messengers left, Jesus began to talk to the crowd about John, when he was preaching and baptizing in the desert. "What did you go out into the desert to see," he asked, "a reed swaying in the wind? Then what did you go to see, a man dressed in fine clothes? A man in fine clothes lives in a palace. Then what did you go out to see, a prophet? Yes, a prophet and more than a prophet. He is the one about who the scriptures say, 'I am sending my messenger ahead of you, he will prepare your way before you.' I tell you that, among men born of women, no one is greater than John; yet the least in the Kingdom of God is greater than he."

Many in the crowd had been baptized by John and were believers, but there were also Pharisees who did not believe; those who were watching Jesus to look for a reason to arrest him. Jesus said to them, "To what shall I compare this generation? They are like children sitting in the marketplace and calling back and forth to each other 'we played the flute for you. but you did not dance!' 'Well, we sang a dirge for you, but you did not weep!' For John came neither eating food nor drinking wine and you said it was because he was possessed. And the Son of Man came eating food and drinking wine and you said it was because he is a glutton and a drunkard. But wisdom is vindication for all her children."

## Forgiveness of a Sinful Woman
From the Good News According to Luke

A Pharisee named Simon invited Jesus to a banquet at his house. Now there was a sinful woman in the town who heard that Jesus was in the house of the Pharisee. She went into the house carrying a flask filled with ointment. Deeply sobbing, she knelt and embraced Jesus' feet, washing them with her tears. Then she dried them with her hair, kissed them, and rubbed the ointment onto them.

Upon seeing this, the Pharisee said, "If this man were really a prophet, he would know what kind of a sinful woman this is who he is allowing to touch him."

Jesus replied, "Simon, I have something to tell you."

"Go on," said Simon.

Jesus said, "Two people were in debt to the same man. One owed five hundred days wages and the other owed fifty. Neither could repay their debt, so the man forgave them both. Which will love the man more?"

"I suppose," said Simon, "that it would be the man with the bigger debt."

"You suppose correctly," said Jesus. Then he turned to the woman and said to Simon, "Do you see this woman? When I entered your house, you did not give water for my feet which is customary, but she has washed them with her tears and dried them with her hair. You did not greet me with a customary kiss, but she has not stopped kissing my feet. You did not anoint my head with oil, but she anointed my feet with ointment. So, I tell you, her many sins are forgiven since she has shown me great love. But to one who loves little, little is forgiven."

Some others at the table were scandalized that Jesus dared to forgive sins. But he said to the woman, "Your faith has saved you, go in peace."

## Some Parables
From the Good News According to Matthew

Jesus taught on the shores of the Sea of Galilee, often using parables. A parable is a lesson wrapped in a story.

He said, "A farmer went out to plant. When he spread the seed, some fell on the footpath. The birds came and ate those. Some fell on rocky ground. They began to grow but soon died because there was not enough soil for their roots to draw water. Some fell among thorns. The thorns grew around them and choked them. But some fell on good, fertile soil. They grew good fruit; sixty or a hundred-fold. Whoever has ears should hear this."

His followers said to him, "Master, why do you teach the crowds in parables?"

He said, "Knowledge of the Kingdom of Heaven has been given to you but not to them. They look but do not see and hear but do not listen. This is to fulfill the prophesy of Isaiah when he said, 'You shall hear but not listen, you shall look but not see.' The people hardly hear with their ears, they have closed their eyes, so they do not understand with their hearts and are not converted and healed.

"But your eyes are blessed for they see, and your ears are blessed for they hear. Many prophets and righteous people have longed to see what you see and hear what you hear.

"So, this is the explanation of the Parable of the Farmer: The seed that fell on the footpath is one who hears the word but does not understand it. The Evil One comes and steals away what is planted in his heart. The seed that fell on rocky ground is the one who hears the word and receives it joyfully at first. But its roots are not deep; when some trouble or persecution comes, he quickly falls away. The seed that fell among the thorns is one who hears the word but then the troubles of life or the lure of wealth choke out the word and he bears no fruit. But the seed that fell on good ground is the one who hears the word and understands it. He will yield good fruit; sixty, or a hundred-fold."

He taught another parable saying, "The Kingdom of Heaven is like a farmer who planted good wheat seeds in his field. When he was asleep his enemy came and planted weeds all around the field and then he went away. When the crop began to grow the weeds grew up among the wheat. When his workers saw the weeds they said to the farmer, 'Didn't you plant good seeds in this field? Where have all the weeds come from?' He said to them, 'My enemy has done this.' The workers said, 'Do you want us to go and pull up the weeds?' He said, 'No, if you pull up the weeds, you might also pull up the wheat along with them. Let them grow together until harvest. At harvest time you will gather the weeds and tie them into bundles for burning. But the wheat, you will gather into my barn.'"

Then he said, "The Kingdom of Heaven is like a mustard seed that someone planted. It is the smallest of seeds, yet, when grown it is the largest of plants. So large that birds come and roost in its branches."

He also said, "The Kingdom of Heaven is like a bit of yeast that a woman put into a tub of dough. Soon all the dough rose and was leavened."

After he dismissed the crowd he went into the house where he was staying. Some of his followers came with him and asked him to explain the parable of the weeds in the field.

He said, "The one who plants good seeds is the Son of Man. The field is the world. The good seeds are the children of the Kingdom. The weeds are the children of the Evil One and the enemy who plants them is Satan. The harvest is the end of the world and the workers are angels. Just as weeds are collected and burned, so it will be at the end of this age. The Son of Man will send his angels and they will take out of his kingdom all those who do evil and cause others to do evil. They will throw them into the fiery furnace where there will be wailing and grinding of teeth. Then the righteous will shine like the sun in the kingdom of their Father."

He told them more parables saying, "The Kingdom of Heaven is like a treasure buried in a field. When someone finds it, he is filled with joy and he re-buries it. Then he sells all that he has and buys the field. The Kingdom of Heaven is like a merchant who shops for pearls. When he finds a pearl of great price, he sells all he has and buys the pearl. Again, the kingdom of Heaven is like a net thrown into the sea that collects all kinds of fish. When it is full, they haul it onto the beach and take the good fish and keep them. The bad fish are thrown away. So it will be at the end of this age; the angels will go out and separate the good from the bad and the bad will be thrown into the furnace.'

"Do you understand these things?" he asked. They said, "yes."

## Jesus Calms the Sea
From the Good News According to Mark

That evening Jesus said to his followers, "Let's cross over to the other side of the sea of Galilee." So, Jesus went with some of them in one boat while others went in some other boats. While they traveled, night came, and Jesus fell asleep on a cushion in the back of the boat. Soon a squall came up and, though the Sea of Galilee is only about twelve miles across, the squall was so violent that the wind buffeted the boat and water began splashing over the sides and filling the boat.

Jesus remained asleep. His followers were terrified. They woke Jesus saying, "Teacher, don't you care that we are about to die?"

Jesus woke up and said to the storm, "Quiet! Be still!" The wind stopped and there was great calm. Then he said to them, "Why were you so afraid? Do you still lack faith?"

They were filled with great awe and said among themselves, "Who is this whom even the wind and sea obey?"

## Exorcism of Legion
From the Good News According to Mark

They arrived at the other side of the sea in a territory called Gerasa. The people of this territory were not Jews but were pagans of mostly Greek descent. The Jews usually avoided them.

As soon as Jesus got out of the boat, a man who was possessed came up to him from some nearby tombs. He had been living among the tombs and no one could subdue him. He had been caught and chained several times but each time he broke the chains and smashed the shackles. Day and night, he would wander among the tombs and nearby hillsides crying out and bruising himself with stones. When he saw Jesus from a distance, he ran to him and fell to the ground before him, crying in a loud voice, "What have you to do with me Jesus, Son of The Most High God? I beg you by your God, do not torment me!"

"What is your name?" asked Jesus.

Legion is my name," said the man, "for we are many." And he pleaded and begged Jesus not to be driven back to Hell.

Now there was a large herd of pigs nearby, feeding on the hillside.

"Please!' begged the man, "Send us into the pigs. Let us enter them!"

Jesus allowed it and the demons came out of the man and went into the pigs. At once the herd of pigs, about two thousand, ran down the steep bank and into the sea and they all drowned.

Upon seeing this, the pig herders ran away and told others what they had seen. The people came out to see for themselves. As they approached Jesus, they saw the man who had been possessed by Legion, sitting there, clothed and in his right mind. This frightened the people. Those among them who saw what had happened explained what Jesus had done. The people were more afraid, and they pleaded with Jesus to leave their district. The man who was healed begged to go with Jesus, but Jesus told him to go back to his family and announce to them all that the Lord in His pity had done. The man did so, and he spread the news of what Jesus had done throughout the ten cities of that district; and all were amazed.

## The Healing of the Daughter of Jairus and the Woman with a Hemorrhage
From the Good News According to Luke

When Jesus returned to Galilee, a crowd came out to greet him. A man named Jairus, an official at the synagogue, came forward and begged Jesus to come to his house because his twelve-year-old daughter was dying. As Jesus followed Jairus, people crowded in on him and it was hard to go forward.

In the crowd was a woman who had a hemorrhage that had not stopped bleeding for twelve years. She had spent all her money on doctors, but they could not heal her. She came up behind Jesus and touched his cloak and her bleeding immediately stopped.

"Who touched me?" said Jesus, "I felt power go out from me."

Though she tried to go away, she could not because of the crowd. She fell to her knees before him and explained what had happened.

"Daughter, your faith has saved you," said Jesus. "Go in peace."

As he was speaking, a messenger came to Jairus and said, "There is no need to trouble the teacher now. Your daughter has died."

When Jesus heard this he said, "Do not worry. Have faith and she will be saved." When he came into the house all the people were crying. Jesus said, "Do not cry. She is not dead, but asleep." They scolded him because they knew she was dead. He took Peter, John, James, and the girl's parents and led them into the room where she was. He took her by the hand and said, "Little girl, get up." Immediately she began to breathe, and she got up.

## The Twelve Are Sent
From the Good News According to Matthew

Jesus summoned the men that would be called The Twelve Apostles. He sent them out over the countryside saying, "Do not go into pagan or Samaritan territory; but, only to the lost sheep of the house of Israel. As you go, proclaim that the Kingdom of Heaven is at hand. Cure the sick, raise the dead, drive out demons. Charge nothing. Take no money nor a pack, nor an extra tunic, nor extra sandals. Whatever town or village you enter look for a good person and stay at that house until you leave. When you enter a house, wish it peace. If a place refuses to hear you, leave there and shake its dust from your sandals. It will be better for Sodom and Gomorrah on the last day than for that place.

"I am sending you like sheep among wolves. Be as shrewd as serpents and as gentle as doves. Beware, for some will hand you over to the courts and whip you, and you will be brought before governors and kings to witness to the pagans. Do not worry about what you will say. You will, at that moment, be given the words to say. Brother will rise against brother and father against child. You will be hated because of my name, but those who endure to the end will be saved. All that is hidden shall be revealed. What I say to you in darkness you will speak in the light. What I whisper, you shout from the hilltops. Do not fear those who can kill the body but not the soul; rather fear the one who can destroy body and soul in Hell. Remember, not one sparrow falls to the ground without your Father's knowledge. He even knows all the hairs of your head. So be not afraid, for you are worth more than many sparrows. Everyone who acknowledges me before others, I will acknowledge before my Heavenly Father.

"Do not think that I have come to bring peace upon the earth. I have not come to bring peace, but a sword. A man will be against his father, a daughter against her mother, and a daughter-in-law against her mother-in-law. Whoever loves father or mother, or son or daughter more than me is not worthy of me. Whoever does not take up his cross and follow me is not worthy of me.

"Whoever finds his life will lose it, and whoever loses his life for my sake will find it. Whoever receives you, receives me and whoever receives me, receives the one who sent me."

Then he sent them out.

When the twelve returned to Galilee, they reported to Jesus everything they had done. They had indeed healed the sick, driven out demons, and raised the dead.

## The Death of John the Baptist
From the Good News According to Mark

Now John the Baptist had earlier been arrested by King Herod because John had criticized Herod for marrying Herodias, his brother's wife. Herodias wanted John dead for offending her, but Herod feared John because John was a holy man.

One day Herod threw himself a birthday feast and invited all his courtiers and military officers and the leading citizens of Galilee. At this feast, the daughter of Herodias performed a dance. Herod was so enraptured by the movements of his stepdaughter that he promised, then and there, to give her whatever she asked for, even up to half his kingdom. The girl went out and asked her mother what she should ask for.

"Ask for the head of the Baptist," said Herodias.

The girl hurried back to the banquet and said, "I want you to give me the head of John the Baptist on a platter, now."

Herod was shocked but, because he had given his word in front of so many people, he sent an executioner with orders to bring back John's head. The man went to the prison and cut off John's head and brought it back on a platter and gave it to the girl. The girl took it and brought it to her mother.

John's followers came to the prison and took his body and laid it in a tomb.

# 4

# You Are the Messiah, the Son of the Living God

## Third Year

*Know that The Lord works miracles for the faithful; The Lord hears when I call. Be moved in your soul and do not sin; ponder in the silence of your rooms. Offer worthy sacrifices and trust in The Lord."*

*Psalm 4*

## The feeding of the Five Thousand
From the Good News According to John

One day, a crowd of about five thousand men, not counting women and children, was following Jesus. He went up to a hilltop by the Sea of Galilee and sat down.

When Jesus saw the size of the crowd, he said to Philip, "where can we buy enough food for them to eat?" though he already knew what he was going to do.

Philip answered, "Two hundred day's wages would not be enough for everyone to have even a little food."

Then Andrew, Simon's brother said, "There is a boy here with five barley loaves and two fish; but what good are they with so many people?"

"Have the people sit," said Jesus.

It was a wide, grassy place so the people sat on the grass. Then Jesus took the loaves, gave thanks to God, and began to pass them out and the fish also. And there were so many loaves, and so many fish, that everybody ate their fill.

When all had eaten, Jesus said, "Gather the leftovers so nothing will be wasted." And when they had done so, there were twelve baskets full of leftover bread from the five loaves the boy had given to Jesus.

When the people saw this, they proclaimed him to be the Messiah and they were going to carry him off and make him king, but Jesus left and went away to be alone.

## Walking on Water
From the Good News According to Matthew

That evening, Jesus told some of his followers to get in their boat and go to Capernaum ahead of him while he prayed alone. When the boat was a few miles offshore the wind blew up against it and it was tossed about and made no headway. Hours after sunset they looked out over the water and saw the figure of a man approaching, walking on the water. They thought it was a ghost and were terrified.

"Don't be afraid," said Jesus. "It is me."

"Lord," said Simon, "if it is you, command me to come to you out on the water."

"Come," said Jesus.

Simon got out of the boat and began to walk on the water toward Jesus, but when he saw how strong the wind was and realized what he was doing, he began to sink and cried out "Lord, save me!"

Jesus reach out and caught him saying, "Oh you of little faith, why did you doubt?"

When they got into the boat the wind quieted and they found themselves at Capernaum.

## The Bread of Life Discourse
From the Good News According to John

The next day, the remnants of the crowd Jesus fed with the loaves and fishes realized that he and his followers had gone. Many of them went to

Capernaum in search of Jesus. They found him teaching in the synagogue and they said to him, "Teacher, when did you get here?"

Jesus replied, "You are not looking for me because of the signs you saw but because I fed you with the loaves and fish. Do not work for food that perishes but for food that gives eternal life which I, the Son of Man, will give you. It is the will of God that you believe in the one whom He sent."

They said to him, "What sign can you give so that we will believe in you? Moses gave our ancestors manna in the desert."

Jesus said, "It was not Moses but God who gave the bread from heaven. The true bread of God comes down from heaven and gives life to the world."

They said to him, "Sir, give us this bread."

Jesus said, "I am the bread of life. Whoever comes to me will not hunger and whoever believes in me will not thirst. For the will of my Father is that everyone who sees the Son and believes will have eternal life, and I will raise him up on the last day."

Many of the people murmured because Jesus said that he was the bread of life.

Jesus told them, "Stop murmuring. Your ancestors ate manna in the desert, but they still died. I am the living bread come down from heaven, whoever eats of this bread will not die but will have eternal life and the bread that I give is my flesh for the life of the world."

The people grew distressed and quarreled among themselves saying, "How can this man give us his own flesh to eat?"

Jesus said, "I tell you, unless you eat the flesh of the Son of Man and drink his blood, you do not have life within you. Whoever eats my flesh and drinks my blood will have eternal life and I will raise him up on the last day. My flesh is true food and my blood is true drink. Whoever eats my flesh and drinks my blood remains in me and I in him."

Many of the people, and even Jesus' followers were bewildered and confused. "This is a hard saying," they said.

"Does this shock you?" asked Jesus, "What if you were to see me, The Son of Man, ascending to where I was before? The words I have spoken to you are spirit and life, yet some among you do not believe."

At these words, many of the crowd went away and even many of his followers left him and went back to their old way of life.

Jesus questioned the Twelve, "Do you also want to leave me?"

"Lord, where would we go?" said Simon, "You have the words of eternal life. We have come to believe, and we know, that you are the Holy One of God."

## The Canaanite Woman's Faith
From the Good News According to Matthew

From there, Jesus and the Twelve went to the region of the Phoenicians who were of Canaanite descent. A Canaanite woman called out to him, "Have pity on me, Son of David! My daughter is tormented by a demon."

"I was sent only to the lost sheep of the house of Israel," Jesus said.

But the woman came up to him and knelt before him saying, "Lord, help me."

Jesus said, "It is not right to take the food of the children and toss it to the dogs."

"Lord," she said, "even the dogs eat the scraps that fall from the master's table."

Then Jesus said to her, "Oh woman, you have great faith. It is done for you as you have asked." And from that very hour, the woman's daughter was healed.

## Jesus Proclaims the Rock
From the Good News According to Matthew

They went to the region of Caesarea Philippi which was a Roman town near Phoenicia. There, Jesus asked the Twelve, "Who do people say that the Son of Man is?"

They answered, "Some say John the Baptist. Others say Elijah. Some say Jeremiah or one of the other prophets."

Then Jesus said, "But, who do you say that I am?"

Simon said, "You are the Messiah, the Son of the Living God."

Jesus said to him, "Blessed are you Simon, son of Jonah, for flesh and blood has not revealed this to you, but my Father in heaven. And so, I proclaim that

130

you are the Rock, and upon this Rock I will build my Assembly, and the gates of Hell shall not stand against it. I will give you the keys to the Kingdom of Heaven. Whatever you bind on Earth shall be bound in Heaven, and whatever you loose on Earth shall be loosed in Heaven." From that time on, until this day, Simon was called The Rock, which in Greek was Petra, and in English, Peter.

Jesus then told his followers that he must go to Jerusalem and suffer at the hands of the elders, chief priests, and scribes and die and be raised on the third day. But they did not yet understand.

## The Transfiguration
From the Good News According to Matthew

After several days, Jesus took The Rock along with James and his brother John and led them up a high mountain. There the face of Jesus shone like the sun and his clothes became as white as light. And Moses and Elijah appeared next to him and began to converse with him about his leaving the earth which he would do in Jerusalem. Then the Rock said to him, "Lord, it is good that we are here. If you like, we can set up three tents here; one for you, one for Moses, and one for Elijah."

But, while he was talking, a bright cloud appeared, and it cast a shadow over them. And a voice from the cloud said, "This is my beloved son, with whom I am well pleased. Listen to him."

When the three men heard this, they were terrified, and they dropped to the ground and hid their faces. But Jesus came over to them and touched them and said, "Get up and do not be afraid." And when they looked up, there was no one there but Jesus.

Jesus commanded them not to tell anyone of this until The Son of Man is raised from the dead.

## The Greatest in the Kingdom of Heaven
From the Good News According to Matthew

After that, they returned to the other followers. A man came up to him saying, "Lord, have pity on my son for he is insane and suffers greatly.

He often falls into the fire and then into the water. I brought him to your followers, but they could not cure him."

Jesus said, "Oh, faithless and perverted generation, how long must I endure you? Bring the boy to me." Jesus scolded the boy and a demon came out of him and from that moment he was healed.

Then his followers asked him in private, "Lord why couldn't we cure the boy?"

Jesus told them, "It is because you have so little faith. I tell you, if you had faith the size of a mustard seed you could say to this mountain 'move' and it would move."

They returned to Capernaum where some of his followers approached him and asked him, "Lord, who is the greatest in The Kingdom of Heaven?"

Jesus called a child over and said to them, "Truly I tell you, if you do not become like children, you will not enter The Kingdom of Heaven. Whoever humbles himself like this child will be the greatest in The Kingdom of Heaven. And whoever is kind to a child such as this, is kind to me. Whoever causes one of these little ones who believe in me to sin, it would be better for him to have a boulder tied around his neck and to be tossed into the sea. See that you always care for little ones such as this for their angels in Heaven always look upon the face of my Father."

Then he said, "If a man has a hundred sheep and one of them wanders off, will he not leave the ninety-nine and go in search of the one? And when he finds it, he rejoices in the one more than in the ninety-nine. In just the same way, it is the will of your Heavenly Father that none of these little ones be lost."

Then Jesus began to instruct them regarding their duty as leaders of his people. He said, "If one of my followers sins, go and tell him his fault just between the two of you. If he does not listen to you, take one or two others along with you and talk to him. If he still refuses to listen, then tell it to the Assembly. If he refuses to listen even to the Assembly, treat him as an outcast. Remember; what you bind on Earth shall be bound in Heaven and what you loose on Earth shall be loosed in Heaven. If two of you agree on

Earth over what to pray about it shall be granted to them. For where two or three of you are gathered in my name, I am there among you."

Then the Rock said to him, "Lord, if one of us offends me how many times should I forgive him; seven times?"

And Jesus said, "Not seven times but seventy-seven times. That is why the Kingdom of Heaven can be likened to a king who decided to settle accounts with his debtors. One debtor who came before him owed him a huge amount that he could never repay. So, the king ordered that he and his family should be sold as slaves to pay the debt. The man fell before him and begged him to have patience and he would repay the debt. At that, the king was filled with compassion and he forgave the man the entire debt.

"When that man left, he saw another man who owed him a much smaller amount. He grabbed the man and started choking him and demanded that he pay the debt. The other man fell to his knees and begged him to be patient, but the first man refused and had the man put into prison.

"When the people saw what had happened, they went to the king and told him about it. The king summoned the man and said to him, 'You evil man! I forgave you your entire debt because you begged me to. Should you not have pity on your debtor as I had pity on you?'

"Then, in his anger, the king had the man handed over to the torturers until he should pay back the entire debt. So will my Heavenly Father do to you unless you forgive each other from your heart."

## The Feast of Booths
From the Good News According to John

The time came for the Feast of Booths when the people set up tents or booths and lived in them for a week to commemorate their ancestors' wanderings in the desert after being set free from Egypt. Many people would spend this time in Jerusalem because it was a time of festival and a chance to bring a sacrifice to the temple. Jesus and his followers also went to Jerusalem even though they knew that many of the priests and temple elders in Jerusalem wanted to kill him. Most of the elders and priests were of the party of the Pharisees or of the party of the Sadducees.

When the feast days were half over, Jesus went and began to teach in the temple courtyard where he attracted the attention of the elders. When the people saw him confronting the elders they wondered if he might truly be the Messiah. But some said that when the Messiah comes no one will know where he is from, but they know where Jesus came from.

Jesus said to them loudly, so all could hear, 'You know me and where I am from. Yet, I came from the one who sent me, and him you do not know. I know him because I am from him and he sent me."

Then the elders sent men over to arrest him, but they did not touch him.

On the last day of the feast, Jesus stood up again in the temple and said, "Let anyone who thirsts come to me and drink, for as scripture says, 'rivers of living water will flow from within him.'"

Some of the crowd who heard his teachings said, "This is a prophet." Others said, 'No, this is the Messiah." While others questioned how a Galilean could be the Messiah when it was known that the Messiah would be a descendant of David. Seeing this public dispute as an excuse, the priests and elders again sent guards to arrest Jesus. When the guards returned without him, they asked why.

The guards said, "We have never heard anyone speak as he does."

"Have you also been tricked?" said the priests. "Does anyone in authority or do any of the Pharisees believe him? The ignorant crowd who believe him are fools." Then they went their separate ways in frustration.

That evening, Jesus went to the Mount of Olives which was a hillside covered with olive orchards across the valley from Jerusalem. It was a place where he often went to pray when he was in Jerusalem.

Early the next morning he went back to the temple courtyard and a great crowd assembled to hear him. He sat down and began to teach them.

Then some scribes and Pharisees brought a woman before him and made a great show, forcing her to stand in the middle of the crowd. They said to him, "Teacher, this woman was caught in the very act of adultery! The Law of Moses says she must be stoned to death. What do you say?"

They were trying to trick him into either condemning a poor woman to death, or into encouraging people to break the Law.

Jesus said nothing but began to write on the ground with his finger. So, they pressed him to answer. He stood up and said, "Let him among you who is without sin throw the first stone." Then he sat down again and continued writing.

The accusers could say nothing in response. One by one they just went away; the elders first, and then the rest until there was no one left standing but the woman.

Jesus stood and said to her, "Woman, where are they? Is there no one to condemn you?"

She looked around and said, "No one."

"Then neither do I condemn you," he said. "Now go, and do not sin anymore."


Jesus continued speaking to the crowd saying, "I am the light of the world. Whoever follows me will not walk in darkness but in life giving light."

The few Pharisees still in the crowd said, "You testify for yourself, so your testimony cannot be confirmed."

Jesus said, "You judge by appearances, but I do not judge. Even in your law it is written that the testimony of two can be valid. I testify on my own behalf and so does my Father who sent me; that makes two."

"Where is your father?" they asked.

Jesus said, "You do not know me or my Father. If you knew me, you would also know my Father. You belong to what is below. I belong to what is above. If you do not believe that I AM, you will die in your sins. When you lift up the Son of Man then you will see that I AM. The one who sent me is with me. He has not abandoned me because I always do what is pleasing to him."

Jesus turned to the crowd and said, "If you heed my words you will truly be my followers and you will know the truth and the truth will set you free."

Someone said, "We are children of Abraham and have never been slaves, so how can you set us free?"

Jesus said, "Everyone who sins is a slave to sin. A slave does not stay in a household, but a son does. So, if a son frees you, you will truly be free. If you were truly Abraham's children, you would be doing the deeds of Abraham. But some of you are trying to kill me, a man who has told you the truth spoken by God. Abraham did not do this."

Then someone said, "We are not orphans, God is our father!"

Jesus replied "If God were your father, you would love me, for I came from God and I am here. Your father is the Devil and you do his will. He was a murderer from the beginning and cannot stand truth for there is no truth in him. He is a liar and the father of lies, but because I speak truth, you do not believe me. Can any of you charge me with sin? Whoever belongs to God hears His words; this is why you do not listen, because you do not belong to God.

"If I glorify myself, my glory is worthless. But it is the Father who glorifies me. If I were to say I do not know him, I would be a liar like you. But I do know Him, and I keep his word. Abraham, your ancestor, rejoiced to see my day; he saw it and was glad."

"You are not even fifty years old." said the Pharisees, "Are you saying you have seen Abraham?"

"Truthfully, I tell you, "said Jesus, "before Abraham even was, I AM."

At this they gathered stones to kill him, but he left the temple area. And many of the crowd came to believe in him because of his words.

## Jesus Heals a Blind Man
From the Good News According to John

As Jesus and his followers passed out of the temple area, they saw a blind man. His followers asked him, "Lord, by whose sin was this man born blind, his own, or his parents'?"

"Neither," said Jesus. "It is so the works of God might be made visible through him. We must do the works of God while the day is still here, while I am still here. I am the light of the world."

Then he spat on the ground and made a paste of mud and he smeared the mud on the eyes of the blind man. Then he told him to go and wash in the Pool of Siloam which was for ceremonial washing and baptism before entering the temple area. The man went and washed, and when he came back, he could see.

Now there were people around who knew the man and they asked him how it was that he could see.

He told them, "The one called Jesus made mud and rubbed it on my eyes. Then he told me to wash in the pool and I did and now I can see!"

The Pharisees heard of this and they had the man born blind brought before them. Jesus had cured the man on the Sabbath and doing any work on the Sabbath was forbidden, so they thought they could accuse him of breaking the Law of Moses because; by curing a man on the Sabbath, he worked. They asked the man what happened, and he told them. Some said that Jesus was not from God because he worked on the Sabbath. But others wondered how a sinful man could do such a miracle. So, they asked the man born blind what he thought.

"He is a prophet," said the man.

Then some of them said he was probably not even born blind. So, they summoned his parents and asked them, "Is this your son who you say was born blind? How is it he can see now?"

"Yes, he is our son and he was born blind," they said. "As to how he can see now, ask him."

So, they called the man born blind back and asked him again what had happened.

"I told you once, but you did not listen," he said. "Why do you want to hear it again; do you want to become his followers too?"

They became angry and said, "You are his follower! We are followers of Moses. We know God spoke through Moses, but we don't know where that Jesus man came from."

The man said, "This is very interesting. We know that God does not listen to sinners, but he does listen to the devout. If this man were not from God, he would not be able to do such wonderful signs." At that they banned him from the temple.

When Jesus heard the man was banned from the temple, he found him and said to him, "Do you believe in the Son of Man?

The man said, "Who is the Son of Man, Lord, that I may believe?"

"You have seen him," said Jesus. "He is speaking to you now."

The man dropped to his knees and said, "Yes, Lord, I believe!"

Jesus said, "I came into this world for judgment; so, the blind can see and the sighted be made blind."

Some of the Pharisees nearby said, "We are not blind."

Jesus said to them, "If you were blind, you would have no sin. But since you say you are not blind, your sin remains."

Then he said to them, "Listen to me. Whoever does not enter a sheep pen through the gate, but climbs over the fence, is a thief and a robber. The shepherd enters through the gate. The gatekeeper opens it for him, and he calls his sheep by name and the sheep know his voice and they follow him out. He walks ahead of them and they follow him because they know his voice. But they will not follow a stranger. They will run away from him because they do not know his voice."

Jesus saw they were confused so he said, "I am the gate for the sheep. Others have come before me, but they were thieves and robbers and the sheep did not listen to them. I am the gate. Whoever enters through me will be saved and will find good pasture. I am the good shepherd. A good shepherd lays down his life for his sheep. A hired man, who does not own the sheep will run away when the wolves come. That is because he works for pay and does not care about the sheep. I am the good shepherd and I know my sheep and they know me, just as the Father knows me and I know the Father; and I will lay down my life for my sheep. I lay it down freely, no one takes it from me. I have power to lay it down and power to take it up again."

And the leaders as well as the people debated among themselves as to who Jesus was.

## Traveling and Teaching
From the Good News According to Luke

After the Feast of Booths, Jesus returned to traveling around the region to teach and cure people of their illnesses. He appointed seventy of his followers to go out in pairs to spread the good news of the Kingdom of God to the towns he planned to visit. He told them, "The harvest is plentiful, but the laborers are few, so ask the Harvester to send out laborers. You too, go out. I am sending you out like lambs among wolves. Carry no money, no pack, no extra sandals. Greet no one on the way. In whatever house you enter, pronounce peace upon it. In whatever town you enter, stay in the same house and do not move about from place to place. If a town welcomes you, cure their sick and pronounce the Kingdom of God. If a town does not welcome you, shake its dust from your feet and move on. On the last day, Sodom will receive more mercy than the towns who reject you, for whoever listens to you, listens to me and whoever rejects you rejects me. And whoever rejects me rejects the one who sent me.

So, they went out to the cities and towns and when they returned to Jesus, they told him, "Lord, even the demons are subject to us because of your name!"

Jesus said to them, "I have seen Satan fall like lightning from the sky. I have given you power to step on snakes and scorpions and on the full force of the enemy and to go unharmed. But do not celebrate because the spirits are subject to you, rather celebrate because your names are written in Heaven. Blessed are the eyes that see what you have seen. For many prophets and kings yearned to see what you see, and hear what you hear, but did not."

A scholar of the Law of Moses stood and said, "Teacher, what must I do to have eternal life?"

Jesus answered, "What does the Law say?"

The man said, "Love the Lord, your God with all your heart, all your soul, all your strength and all your mind, and love your neighbor as yourself."

"You have answered correctly," said Jesus, "Do these things, and you will be saved."

"But who is my neighbor?" asked the man.

Jesus said, "A man was traveling from Jerusalem to Jericho and robbers set upon him. They took all he had, stripped him, beat him, and left him for dead. A priest of the Temple came upon him, but when he saw him, he passed by on the other side of the road. Then a Levite came by, but he also passed on the other side of the road. Then a Samaritan traveler came by and he was moved with pity for the man. He knelt and cleansed his wounds with oil and wine, and he bandaged them. Then he lifted him up onto his own animal and took him to an inn where he comforted him. The next day he gave two silver coins to the innkeeper and said, 'Take care of him, if you spend more than this, I will repay you on my way back.' Now, which of the three men was a neighbor to the man who had been robbed?"

"The man who showed mercy," said the scholar.

"Go and do the same," said Jesus.

As they traveled, they entered a town called Bethesda and went to the house of a friend named Lazarus and his sisters, Martha and Mary. Jesus entered the house and sat and began teaching the assembled people. Mary sat at his feet and listened to everything he said.

Her sister, Martha, had been busy about the house, serving and caring for their guests. After a while she said to Jesus, "Lord, don't you care that my sister has left me to do all the work? Tell her to help me."

Jesus said, "Martha, Martha, you worry about many things. There is need for just one thing. Mary has made the better choice, and it will not be taken from her."

He revealed that he intended to return to Jerusalem for the upcoming Passover. Some Pharisees said to him, "Don't go there because Herod wants to kill you."

Jesus said, "Go and tell that fox that I cast out demons and I perform healings today and tomorrow, and on the third day I accomplish my purpose. Yet, I must go to Jerusalem for it is impossible that a prophet should die outside Jerusalem."

## Other Parables
From the Good News According to Luke

Jesus said, "A man had two sons. The younger son said to his father, 'Father, give me my inheritance now.' So, the father divided his property between his sons. After a few days, the younger son took his inheritance and went to a foreign country where he spent it on entertainment and bad living. When he had spent it all, a famine came upon that country and he was in dire need. So, he took a job on a farm tending pigs. He longed to fill his belly on the food the pigs ate, but no one gave him any. Finally, he came to his senses and said to himself, 'My father's servants have food enough to eat but here I am dying of hunger. I will go to my father. I will tell him I have sinned and no longer deserve to be called his son. I will ask him to hire me as a servant.' So, he left and went to his father's house. As he approached, his father saw him from a distance and was filled with compassion. He ran out to his son and threw his arms around him and kissed him. His son said, 'Father, I have sinned against heaven and you. I no longer deserve to be called your son.' But the father called to his servants, 'Hurry, and bring the finest robe for him! Put a ring on his finger and sandals on his feet. Take the fattest calf and slaughter it and let us celebrate with a feast because my son was dead and has come back life! He was lost but now is found!' Then the celebration began. Now the older son had been out in the fields, and when he came back to the house, he heard music and dancing. He called to one of the servants to ask what was going on and the servant said, 'Your brother has returned, and your father is throwing a feast because his son is back, safe and sound.' The older brother grew angry and would not even enter the house. So, the father went out to plead with him to come in, but he said, 'Listen Father, all these years I worked for you and did everything you ask; yet, you never even gave me a young goat to feast with my friends. But when that son returns after spending all your money on prostitutes, you slaughter a fat calf for him!' The father said, 'My son, you have always been my comfort and everything I have is yours. But now is the time to celebrate because your brother was dead and has come to life; he was lost and has been found.'"

Jesus told them another parable saying, "There was a rich man who dressed in fine clothes and ate wonderful food every day. Lying at his door was a poor man named Lazarus, covered with sores. He would gladly have eaten from the scraps that fell from the rich man's table. Dogs would come and lick his wounds. When the poor man died, angels came and carried him away into the embrace of Abraham. The rich man died and, from the underworld where he was in torment, he looked up and saw Abraham far off and Lazarus at his side. He cried out, 'Father Abraham, have pity on me. Send Lazarus to dip the tip of his finger in water and cool my tongue, for I am suffering in these flames.' Abraham answered, 'My son, remember you had all good things in life while Lazarus had the bad. Moreover, there is a wide chasm between us that was established so no one can pass from one side to the other.' 'Then I beg you father,' said the rich man, 'send him to my father's house for I have five brothers. He could warn them, so they don't come to this place of torment.' But Abraham replied, 'They have Moses and the prophets. They should listen to them.' And the rich man said, 'Oh no Father Abraham, but if someone from the dead tells them, they will change their ways.' But Abraham said, 'If they do not listen to Moses and the prophets, they will not listen even if someone were to rise from the dead.'

## The Raising of Lazarus
From the Good News According to John.

Jesus returned to Galilee, but Lazarus, the brother of Martha and Mary fell ill in the village of Bethany, so the sisters sent word to Jesus saying, "Master, your beloved friend is sick."

When he had heard this, Jesus said, "This illness will not end in death, but is so the Son of God may be glorified through it." And he stayed where he was for two days. Then he told his followers he was going back to Bethany. Now Bethany was in Judea just a short walk from Jerusalem, so his followers tried to discourage him from going near Jerusalem since the elders had tried to stone him in the temple.

Then Jesus said, "Our friend Lazarus sleeps. I go to wake him."

And they said, "Lord, if he is asleep then he is fine."

Then Jesus said, "Lazarus has died. I am glad for your sake that I was not there, so you can believe. Now we go to him."

Thomas said to the others, "Let us go with him to die with him."

When Jesus arrived at Bethany, Lazarus had been dead and in his tomb for four days. Many people had come to comfort Martha and Mary over the loss of their brother.

When Martha heard that Jesus was approaching, she went out to him while Mary stayed in the house. "Lord," she said, "if you had been here my brother would not have died. But I know that, even now, God will give you whatever you ask."

"Your brother will rise," said Jesus.

"Yes Lord," she said. "I know he will rise in The Resurrection of all people on the Last Day."

Jesus said, "I am The Resurrection and the life. Whoever believes in me, even if he dies, will live, and all who believe in me will never die. Do you believe this?"

"I do, Lord," she said. "I have come to believe that you are the Messiah, the Son of God, who is coming to the world."

Jesus stayed outside the village and he sent Martha to get her sister. When Martha whispered to Mary that the Teacher was here and wanted to see her, Mary got up and ran to where he was. The people who were with her assumed she was going to mourn at her brother's tomb, and they followed behind her.

When Mary saw Jesus, she began crying as she ran faster. She fell at his feet saying, "Lord, if you had been here, my brother would not have died."

When Jesus saw her weep so much and the people with her weeping, he wept with them. "Where have you laid him?" he said.

"Come and see," said the people, and they led him on; but some were saying "He loved Lazarus so much. Couldn't he, who brought sight to the blind, have done something so Lazarus would not have died?"

Jesus arrived at the tomb. It was a cave with a large stone laying across the entrance. "Remove the stone," he said.

Martha said, "Lord, he has been dead for four days. There will be a stench."

But Jesus said, "Didn't I tell you that, if you believe, you will see the glory of God?"

So, they rolled the stone away.

Jesus raised his eyes and said, "Father, I know you always hear me, but for the sake of the crowd, I speak out loud so that they will believe." Then he cried out in a loud voice, "Lazarus, come out!" And the dead man came out, still tied in burial cloths and with his head covered. Jesus said, "Untie him," which they did, and he was well.

When they had heard of the raising of Lazarus, the head council of the Jews, called the Sanhedrin, met to discuss what to do about Jesus. They were afraid that, if all the people came to believe in him, the Romans would see it as an insurrection and come and take away their nation. One of them named Caiaphas, who was the High Priest that year said, "It is better that one man die instead of all the people." So, from that time on, they agreed to kill him. After this, Jesus no longer went about in public but stayed for a while with his followers in a town called Ephraim near the desert.

## Toward Jerusalem
From the Good News According to Matthew

In Ephraim he was recognized, and a crowd gathered around him and children were brought to him to be blessed, but his followers tried to block them thinking they would bother the Master.

He said to them, "Let the children come to me and do not prevent them, for the Kingdom of Heaven is made of such as these." Then they came to him and he placed his hands on them and blessed them.

Then a rich man came to him and asked, "What must I do to gain eternal life?"

Jesus said, "Keep the commandments. Do not kill, do not commit adultery, do not steal, do not bear false witness, honor your father and your mother."

"I do all that," said the rich man, 'What else must I do?"

Jesus said, "If you wish to be perfect, go and sell all you have and give it to the poor, and you will have treasure in Heaven. Then come and follow me."

When the rich man heard this, he went away sad because he had many things and did not wish for poverty.

Then Jesus said to his followers, "It will be easier for a camel to pass through the eye of a needle than for a rich man to enter the Kingdom of Heaven."

"Then who can be saved?" said the followers.

"For man it is impossible," he said, "but for God all things are possible."

Then the Rock said, "Lord, we have given up everything to follow you. What will be for us?"

Jesus told them, "I say to you who have followed me that, when the Son of Man sits on his throne in glory, you yourselves will sit on twelve thrones, judging the tribes of Israel. And everyone who has given up home and family to follow me will be repaid a hundred times and will inherit eternal life."

The time for the Passover was approaching when the people would gather in Jerusalem to commemorate and celebrate the night when people spread the blood of the lambs on the wood of their doors so that, whoever is marked with the blood of the lamb, death passed over that house and did not enter.

Some of his followers tried to discourage him from going because they knew the elders of the temple wanted to kill him. But he would not be discouraged. So, Jesus and the Twelve, and the other followers, including Mary, his mother, and Mary of Magdala, went up to Jerusalem. As they went, Jesus took the Twelve aside and told them, "We are going to Jerusalem, and the Son of Man will be handed over to the chief priests and the scribes and they will condemn him to death, and will hand him over to the Romans to be mocked, and whipped, and crucified, and he will rise on the third day."

The mother of James and John, the sons of Zebedee came to Jesus and asked if, when he comes into his kingdom, her sons could sit at his right hand and his left hand.

"You do not know what you are asking," he said. 'Can you drink the cup I am to drink?"

They said, "we can."

He said, "You will indeed drink of the same cup. But to sit at my right and left hand, that has already been prepared by my Father."

When the other ten heard this, they became indignant at James and John, so Jesus called them together and said, "You know the rulers of the Romans lord over them and make their authority felt. But it will not be so among you. Whoever wishes to be great among you, must be the servant. Whoever wished to be first, must be as a slave. The Son of Man did not come to be served but to serve, and to give his life as a ransom for many."

# 5

# Love One Another as I Have Loved You

## *The Last Week*

*The stone the builders rejected has become the corner stone. The Lord has done this, and it is wonderful to see. Lord, grant salvation.*
*Psalm 118*

**Entry into Jerusalem**
From the Good News According to Matthew, Mark, Luke and John

Six days before Passover, Jesus came to the house of Lazarus and his sisters in Bethany. They gave a dinner for him and the Twelve and, while Martha served and Lazarus ate, Mary took an expensive bottle of perfumed oil and rubbed it on Jesus' feet and dried them with her hair and she poured some over his head, filling the room with the smell of perfume.

Then Judas Iscariot, the one of the Twelve who would betray him, said, "That oil could have been sold for three hundred days' wages and the money given to the poor." He did not say this because he cared for the poor but because he was in charge of the money bag and would steal from it.

"Leave her alone," said Jesus, "Why do you criticize her? You will always have the poor with you, but you will not always have me. She has anticipated my burial. Let her keep what is left to anoint my corpse. I tell

147

you, wherever the good news of me is told throughout the world, what she has done for me will be told to her honor."

The next day was the time for Jesus to enter Jerusalem. He was accompanied by the Twelve and many other followers, and many onlookers. They were on the Mount of Olives across the valley from the city. He told two followers, "Go into that village and in it you will find a tethered donkey colt which has never been sat on. Untie it and bring it here. If anyone asks you what you are doing say 'The Master needs it.'"

The two went and found everything just as Jesus said they would. As they were untying the colt, its owner asked them what they were doing, and they said, "The Master needs it," and he let them go.

They brought the colt to Jesus, threw their cloaks over it, and helped him mount it. There were people there who had seen Jesus raise Lazarus and they spread the news saying, "Jesus of Nazareth is here!" and people came from the countryside and poured out of the city to welcome him. A great crowd lined both sides of the road all the way into Jerusalem. People were throwing their cloaks on the road before the colt. Many had gone out and cut green branches and palm branches; some they waved in the air, others they tossed on the road as Jesus approached, making a carpet of cloaks and palm branches as was done for kings. Jesus rode down one slope of the valley and up the other slope toward the gates of Jerusalem, riding a donkey colt just as the prophecy had said; "Say to daughter Jerusalem, see your king comes to you, gentle and riding on a donkey, the foal of a beast of burden."

The multitude began to joyfully shout "Hosanna!" which means, Lord, grant salvation!" They shouted, "Blessed is he who comes in the name of the Lord! It is the king! Blessed is the kingdom of our father David which is to come! Lord, grant salvation in the highest!"

Some Pharisees in the crowd shouted to Jesus, "Teacher admonish your followers!"

He said, "I tell you, if they kept quiet, these stones would cry out!"

As he passed through the gates the Pharisees said to one another, "See how we win nothing. Look, the whole world is following him."

Jesus entered the city and passed through the crowds to the temple courtyard. There he saw the money changers and animal sellers hard at work, cheating and overcharging the people for the privilege of offering sacrifices at Passover. So, as he had done before, he disrupted their business, turning over their tables and saying, "It is written 'My house shall be a house of prayer' but you have made it a den of thieves!"

Still, the elders did not move against him because of the crowd who loved him. Instead, blind and crippled people came up to him and he cured them. And children were hollering, "praise to the Son of David, the Messiah!" This was all much to the distress of the elders, the scribes, and the Pharisees.

When evening came, Jesus and his followers returned to Bethany for the night.

## Jesus and the Temple Elders
From the Good News According to Matthew

The next day Jesus returned to the temple and began teaching the people. Some chief priests came to him and said, "By whose authority do you do what you do? Who gave you that authority?"

"I will ask you one question," said Jesus, "and if you answer it, I will tell you by whose authority I do what I do. Tell me; John's baptism, was it from Heaven or from Earth?"

They conversed among themselves saying that if they said it was from Heaven then Jesus would ask them why they did not believe in him, but if they say it was from Earth, the people will be angry because they believed in John. Finally, they said, "We do not know."

Jesus said, "Then neither shall I tell you from where my authority comes.

"But let me ask you, what do you think of this? There was a man who had two sons. He said to one son, 'Go out and work in the field today.' The son said no, but later he went out and worked. Then the man said to the second son, 'Go out and work in the field.' That son said yes, but he did not go. Now, which son did the will of his father?"

149

"The first one," answered the priests.

"Yes," said Jesus, "And I tell you that tax collectors and prostitutes are entering the Kingdom of Heaven before you priests and elders because, when John was here, you did not believe him, but tax collectors and prostitutes did."

Then he said, "Let me tell you a story. A landowner planted a vineyard and grew a hedge around it and dug a well and put up a watch tower. Then he leased it out to tenants and went away. When harvest time came, he sent his servants to the tenants to collect his share. But the tenants beat and killed them. So, he sent more servants, but the tenants killed them also. Then the landowner sent his own son, thinking that the tenants will have to respect him. But they took the son and beat him and killed him. What will the landowner do to those tenants when he comes?"

They answered, "He will put those miserable tenants to a miserable end and lease the vineyard out to new tenants who will do his will."

"In the same way," said Jesus, "the Kingdom of God will be taken from you and given to others who will produce its fruit."

This angered the priests, but they were afraid to act in front of the crowd.

Jesus spoke on saying, "You see, the Kingdom of God is like a king who gave a great wedding feast for his son. He sent his servants out to invite chosen guests. Some ignored them. Some refused. Some took the servants and killed them. The king, in his rage, sent his soldiers out and destroyed those who had rejected the invitation.

"Then he said to his servants, 'The feast is all laid out and ready. Go out and invite whoever you meet.' So, they did, and many people came, good and bad, and they filled the wedding hall. But one man who was there showed disrespect by not dressing properly for the feast. When the king asked him why, the man gave no answer. So, the king had him bound and tossed outside into darkness where there is wailing and grinding of teeth. You see, many are invited but few are chosen."

The elders then went away and discussed among themselves how they could trap Jesus with his own words. They hatched a plan by which they thought they could trick him into either supporting the Roman oppressors and alienate the people, or into rejecting the Romans and be liable to treason. They sent some of their servants back to Jesus in the temple.

The servants said to him, "Teacher, we know that you teach the truth and the way of God and that you are not concerned with opinions of others, even those in authority. Tell us then, should we pay taxes to Caesar, the Roman emperor?"

"Why are you trying to trick me you hypocrites?" said Jesus, "Give me a coin."

They handed him a Roman coin and Jesus held it up.

"Whose image is this and whose name is written here?"

"Caesar," they said.

"Then," said Jesus, "give to Caesar what is Caesar's and give to God what is God's"

When they heard this, they were dumbfounded, and they went away.


Shortly thereafter some Sadducees came to him. Many of the priests were Sadducees and this group did not believe in the future resurrection of the dead. They said to him, "Teacher, there were seven brothers. The first married a woman but he died without any children. So, according to the law, the second brother married her so the dead brother could have children through him. But he died without any children. And so, each brother married the woman and died with no children and, finally, the woman died. Now, after the resurrection of the dead, when they are all brought back to life, whose wife will the woman be?"

"Jesus said, "You do not understand because you do not know the scriptures or the power of God. At the resurrection, there is no marriage, but all will be like angels. And concerning the resurrection, have you not read that God said, 'I am the God of Abraham, the God of Isaac, and the God of Jacob'? He is not the god of the dead, but of the living."

Then another Pharisee came to him and said, "Teacher, which is the greatest commandment?"

Jesus said, "You shall love the Lord, your God with all your heart, with all your soul, and all your mind. That is the greatest commandment. And the second is like it: you shall love your neighbor as yourself."

151

Then Jesus turned to the crowd and to his followers and said, "The Scribes and the Pharisees sit on the seat of Moses, so do what they tell you to do, but do not follow their example. By their laws they place heavy burdens on people's shoulders, but they do nothing to lighten them. They love the places of honor at banquets and gatherings, and they love to be called 'teacher' and 'father.' But do not let yourselves be called so, for you are all brothers. You have one father in Heaven. The greatest among you must be the servant. Whoever raises himself will be humbled; whoever humbles himself will be raised."

He turned back to his adversaries saying, 'Shame on you, you Scribes and Pharisees, you hypocrites. You lock people out of the Kingdom of Heaven. You do not even enter it yourselves. You travel over sea and land to make one convert and when you do, you make him a son of Hell even more than yourselves. You blind guides, you hypocrites! You dutifully pay your donations to the temple even down to the spices you grow; but you neglect the weightier things like judgement, and mercy, and faithfulness. You should donate those as well. You strain out the gnat but swallow the camel! Shame on you, you Scribes and Pharisees! You wash the outside of a cup but inside it is full of plunder and self-indulgence. Clean the inside as well as the outside. Shame on you, you Scribes and Pharisees! You are like whitewashed tombs which look beautiful on the outside but inside are full of dead men's bones and filth. You snakes! You brood of vipers! How can you escape the judgement of Hell?

"I will send you prophets and wise men. Some you will kill and crucify, some you will whip in the synagogues so that on you, who should know better, will be all the innocent blood shed upon the earth from the blood of Abel to the blood of the murdered prophets. These things will come upon this generation.

"Oh Jerusalem, Jerusalem! You kill the prophets who are sent to you. How many times I yearned to gather your children as a hen gathers her young under her wing, but you were unwilling! Now your house will be abandoned. But you will see me when you say, 'Blessed is he who comes in the name of the Lord.'" Then he left the temple.

## Jesus Tells of the Fall of Jerusalem and of Future Things
From the Good News According to Luke

As Jesus was leaving the temple area some of his followers were talking about how wonderful the building was. He said, "There will not be a single stone left upon another."

He went back to the Mount of Olives and, as he sat looking out at Jerusalem across the valley, some of his followers asked him what he had meant about the stones of the temple. He said, "Do not let yourselves be fooled for many will come in my name and say 'I am the Messiah,' but they are deceivers. There will be wars and rumors of wars. There will be famines and earthquakes in places. These will be the beginnings of the labor pains. They will persecute and kill you and you will be hated among the nations because of my name. But do not prepare your own defense for I shall give you wisdom when the time comes. Many false prophets will come and deceive many, but those who persevere to the end will be saved and the good news of the Kingdom of God will be preached to all nations, and the end will come.

"When you see Jerusalem surrounded by armies, those in Judea must flee to the mountains. Grief will come to the pregnant and nursing mothers for there will be great tribulation. They will fall by the sword or be taken as slaves for foreigners and Jerusalem will be trampled underfoot.

"There will be signs in the sun and the moon, and the stars and the power of the skies will be shaken, and they will see the Son of Man in clouds and glory and be afraid. But you; stand tall for your redemption is at hand.

"Consider how, when the fig tree sends forth blossoms, you know summer is coming. In the same way, when you see these things happening, you know the Kingdom of God is near. This generation will not pass away before these things happen.

## The Plot Against Jesus
From the Good News According to Matthew

Now, the chief priests and elders of the temple had decided to kill Jesus, but they did not want to arrest him in front of the crowds for they feared a riot. While they were gathered in the house of Caiaphas, the high priest, Judas Iscariot came to them secretly. He was one of the Twelve and had been trusted with the ministry's money. He was a thief, but he was not satisfied with pilfering from his friends. He knew that the priests were looking for a chance to get hold of Jesus. He said, "What will you give me if I hand him over to you?" They paid him thirty pieces of silver and he started looking for an opportunity to hand him over to them.

## The Last Supper
From the Good News According to Matthew, Mark, Luke, and John

When the day for celebrating Passover had come, Jesus sent the Rock and John into the city to prepare for the feast. They asked him where to find a place for their feast and he told them, "When you go into the city you will see a man carrying a jug of water. Follow him. The place where he goes will have a large upper room. That is where you are to prepare for the feast." They went off and found everything as he said, and they prepared the room for the feast.

That night Jesus and his closest followers gathered in the upper room for the feast.

While they were eating Jesus said to them, "I have long waited to celebrate this Passover with you." He got up from the supper table and took off his cloak and tied a towel around his waist. He got a bowl of water and went around to each of them and washed their feet and dried them with the towel. This is something a servant or slave did, not the host of the feast.

When he came to Simon the Rock, the man was scandalized and said, "Lord, are you going to wash my feet?"

Jesus said, "You don't understand this now, but you will later."

"You will never wash my feet!" said the Rock.

Jesus said, "Unless I wash you, you will not have an inheritance with me." So, it was done.

When he had returned to his place at the table he said, "Do you realize what I have done for you? You call me 'teacher' and 'master' and so I am.

Yet since I, the master, have washed your feet like a servant, you should do the same for each other. This is an example for you to follow."

While they were eating, Jesus took bread, blessed it, and broke it, and giving it out to his followers he said, "Take this and eat it; this is my body." Then he took a cup, gave thanks, and passed it to them saying, "Drink this, all of you, for this is my blood of the new covenant which will be shed for you and for many for the forgiveness of sins. Do this in memory of me. I will not drink of the fruit of the vine until I drink it new, with you, in the Kingdom of Heaven."

When they had shared the cup, Jesus became somber and said, "One of you will betray me."

They were shocked. "Not me," they said, 'Not me."

Jesus broke off a piece of bread and said, "The one to whom I give this bread will betray me." He handed it to Judas Iscariot and told him, "Go, and do quickly what you will do." Judas left the room, leaving the others speechless.

Then Jesus said to them all, "Now the Son of Man will be glorified, and God too, through him.

"My children, I will leave you soon. You will look for me but where I am going, you cannot follow. So, I give you a new commandment: love one another as I have loved you. This is how all will know that you are my followers, that you love one another."

The Rock said, "Master, where are you going?"

Jesus answered, "Where I am going, you cannot follow now, though you will follow later."

"Why can't I follow now?" said the Rock, "I would follow you to my death!"

"Would you die for me?" asked Jesus, "I tell you Simon Rock, before the rooster crows in the morning you will deny you know me three times."

Then he addressed them all saying, "Do not worry. You have faith in God so have faith in me. In my Father's house there are many wonderful dwelling places. I go to prepare a place for each of you. I will return and gather you so that where I will be, you all will also be. You already know the way there."

Then Thomas said, "Lord, how do we know the way?"

Jesus said, "I am the way, and the truth, and the life. No one comes to the Father except through me. If you know me then you will know my Father."

Then Philip said, "Master, show us the Father."

Jesus said in reply, "Don't you know that I am in the Father and the Father is in me? The Father speaks through me.

"If you love me, you will keep my commandments and I will ask the Father and He will send you another Advocate to be with you always. It is The Spirit of Truth which the world cannot accept because it does not know the truth. But you will know.

"I will not leave you orphaned. In a little while, the world will no longer see me, but you will see me for I remain in you. You will see that I am in the Father and the Father is in me. I have told you this while I am still here. The Advocate, the Holy Spirit that the Father will send, He will remind you of all that I have told you.

"I am the vine; you are the branches. Whoever remains in me, and I in him, will bear much fruit. My father will be glorified because you will bear much fruit. As the Father loves me, so I love you. If you keep my commandments, you will remain in my love. This is my commandment; love one another as I have loved you. There is no greater love than to lay down one's life for one's friends. You are my friends. You did not choose me, but I chose you and appointed you. You will bear fruit that will remain so that whatever you ask the Father in my name, he will give. So, I command you, love one another.

"If the world hates you, know that it is because it hated me. I took you out of the world, so the world hates you. Those who kept my words will keep yours. But those who persecuted me will persecute you because they do not know me, and they do not know my Father. If I had not done great miracles that no one has ever done before, they would have no blame. But they saw the things I have done and still they hate both me and the Father, so they have no excuse.

"So, now I have told you that I will soon be gone, and you are sad. But I tell you, it is better for you that I go. For if I do not go, the Advocate will not come. I have more to tell you, but you cannot bear it now. But when he comes, The Spirit of Truth, he will guide you to all truth. He will declare to you all that I give to him and all that I give to him is from the Father.

"In a little while you will not see me, but a little while after that you will see me again."

At this, one of them spoke up, "We do not understand what you mean that we will not see you then see you again."

Jesus said, "Soon you will weep while the world celebrates. You will grieve but your grief will become joy. Just as a woman suffers in labor; but, when her child is born, she forgets her pain and rejoices in her child; so, you will rejoice, and I will see you again."

Then Jesus prayed, "Father, the hour has come. I glorified you on Earth by doing what you sent me to do. Now glorify me, Father, with the glory that I had with you before the world began. I revealed you to those whom you gave to me and they have come to believe that you sent me. I pray for them. I have been glorified through them and now I will come to you and leave them in the world. Father keep them in your name so that they can be one as you and I are one. While I was with them, I protected them, but now they will remain in this world to which they no longer belong. So, make them holy. As you sent me, so I now send them so that they may be made holy with the truth.

"I also pray for those who will believe in me through their words, that they may all be one in love with me and with you, so the world may believe."

# 6

# It is Finished

## *The Agony of the Messiah*

*My God, my God, why have you abandoned me? Why so far from my cries? You are the enthroned Holy One, the glory of Israel. In you our ancestors trusted, and you rescued them. To you they cried out and were not disappointed.*

*But I am as a worm; hardly a man. All who see me mock me. They curl their lips and shake their heads. "You relied on the Lord, let him save you. If He loves you, let Him rescue you." Yet you drew me forth from the womb and made me safe at my mother's breast; from birth you are my God. Be near me for trouble is upon me and there is no one to help.*

*Wild bulls surround me. They tear like lions. My life drains away. My heart melts like wax within me. My throat is as dry as fired clay; my tongue clings to my palate; I am in the dust of death.*

*Many dogs surround me; a pack of evil doers close in on me. They have pierced my hands and my feet; I can count all my bones. They gloat at me; they divide my clothes among themselves; for my cloak they throw dice.*

*But you Lord, deliver me. I will proclaim your name to the people. For God has not abandoned me but heard me when I cried out. I will fulfill my vows before those who fear the Lord. The poor will eat their fill; those who seek the Lord will offer praise.*

*All the ends of the Earth will turn to the Lord; the nations will bow before you, for kingship belongs to the Lord. All who sleep in the earth will bow down before the Lord; and I will live for the Lord. Future generations will serve Him, and His deliverance will be preached to people yet unborn.*

*Psalm 22*

## The Arrest of Jesus
From the Good News According to Matthew, Mark, Luke, and John

After the meal, Jesus went with his followers across the valley to the Mount of Olives to a garden called Gethsemane, which means "oil press." He often went there to pray during his stays in Jerusalem. He told his followers to wait for him while he took the Rock and the two brothers, James and John, and went a little farther on. There he said to them, "My soul is filled with deathly sorrow. Wait here and keep watch for me while I go pray."

He went a little farther into the garden and prayed, "My Father, if it is possible, let this cup pass me by. But not my will, but yours be done." He went back and found the three asleep. He said to the Rock, "Simon, you could not stay awake with me even for an hour?" he said, "Stay awake and pray that you may not undergo the final test. The spirit is willing, but the body is weak." He went back to pray some more and when he returned, he found them asleep again. Then he returned to pray. He was in such agony and prayed so fervently that his sweat fell like drops of blood, and an angel came to console and strengthen him. When he rose from prayer, he found the three asleep with grief. "Are you still asleep?" he said, "You should be praying. It is no matter now. The time has come for the Son of Man to be handed over to sinners. Look, my betrayer is here."

As he spoke, Judas came to the garden with a crowd carrying torches and swords and clubs. They were Pharisees and temple guards and servants of the High Priest. Judas had arranged a sign. He had told them that the man he greets with a kiss will be Jesus, the man they were to arrest. He approached Jesus saying, "Teacher," and he kissed him on the cheek.

159

"Judas," said Jesus, "must you betray me with a kiss?"

Then he turned to the crowd and said, "Who are you looking for?"

They said, "Jesus of Nazareth."

Jesus said, "I AM."

At that they all fell to the ground. When they came to their senses, he asked them again, "Who are you looking for?"

Again, they said "Jesus of Nazareth."

"I told you that I am he," said Jesus, "Do what you must do, but let these others go."

Then the Rock drew a sword and cut off the ear of one of the Chief Priest's servants.

"Put away your sword!" said Jesus, "He who lives by the sword, dies by the sword.

Don't you know that I could call on my Father right now and He would send me a great army of angels? But then how would the prophesies be fulfilled that it must happen this way?"

Then Jesus healed the servant's ear. He turned to the crowd and said, "Why have you come after me with swords and clubs like I was a bandit? Day after day I sat in the courtyards of the Temple and preached; yet, you did not arrest me. But it is done this way to fulfill the prophesies."

Then they tied him up while his followers ran away.

## Questioning Before the Sanhedrin
From the Good News According to Matthew

Jesus was taken into the city, to the house of Caiaphas who was high priest that year. Simon The Rock, who had been following at a distance, stopped at the gate of the house. The servants had made a fire in the court-yard because it was cold, and the Rock went in and sat with them at the fire. One of the women servants looked closely at him and said, "You were with that Jesus man."

"I don't know what you are talking about," answered the Rock. And he got up and waited outside the gate.

Caiaphas had gathered the priests, scribes, and elders of the Sanhedrin which was the council of elders of the Temple. They began to question Jesus about his teachings and the things he had done.

"Why are you asking me these things?" he said, "Ask all those who I have taught."

At that, a temple guard hit him in the head saying, "Is that how you answer the high priest?"

Jesus said, "If I have spoken wrongly, say what the wrong was; but if I had spoken rightly, why do you hit me?"

While the Rock was at the gate, the servant woman saw him again and said to some bystanders, "This man is one of them!"

"You are mistaken," said the Rock, "I am not."

Inside, the high priest and the Sanhedrin kept questioning Jesus, trying to get him to testify against himself, but to no avail. Then they produced witnesses who accused Jesus of many things but, since they were lying, their testimony did not agree and could not be relied upon. Finally, Caiaphas stood and said to Jesus, "What do you have to say? Why don't you answer these accusations?" Jesus remained silent, so Caiaphas said, "Are you the Messiah, the son of God?"

"I am," said Jesus, "And you will see me, the Son of Man, seated at the right hand of the One of Power and coming with the clouds of heaven."

Caiaphas tore his own robes in anger and proclaimed, "What need do we have of witnesses? You have heard his blasphemy! What do you all say?" And they all agreed that Jesus should die. They blindfolded him, spat on him, and hit him saying, "Well, prophet, who hit you?" Then they took off the blindfold and led him out to take him to Pontius Pilate who was the Roman governor and who was in town for the Passover, because only the Romans could condemn a man to death.

As they were going out. Some bystanders said to the Rock, "You must be one of them because you talk like a Galilean."

He began to curse and swear and say, "I do not know him! I don't know what you are talking about." Just then a rooster crowed, and Jesus turned and looked at him. When their eyes met, the Rock remembered that Jesus said he would deny him three times before the rooster crowed. He ran away weeping bitterly.

## Questioning of the Governor and the Prince
From the Good News According to Matthew and Mark

At daybreak, the priests and elders brought Jesus to Pontius Pilate. They accused Jesus of misleading the people, of opposing Roman taxes, and of claiming to be the Messiah. Pilate questioned him briefly but found no guilt in him. When they said he had been causing trouble in Galilee, Pilate, happy to be rid of this annoyance, ordered Jesus sent to Herod, who was also in Jerusalem for the Passover, because Herod was the prince of Galilee.

Herod, the son of the Herod who had ordered the baby boys in Nazareth to be killed when Jesus was born, was happy to see Jesus. He had heard of his miracles and hoped Jesus would perform one for him. He questioned Jesus at length, but Jesus gave no reply. Then he and his men began to make fun of Jesus. They dressed him up like a king and sent him back to Pilate.

Caiaphas and the elders brought Jesus back to the Roman barracks where Pilate was staying. They stood in the courtyard and Pilate came out to them and stood on the steps. 'What are the charges against him?" Pilate asked.

They said, "If he were not a criminal, we wouldn't have brought him to you."

"Then take him away and judge him according to your own laws," said Pilate.

They said, "We need your authority to execute him."

So, Pilate went back inside and had Jesus brought with him. "Are you the king of the Jews?" he said.

"Is this your own question," said Jesus, "or have others told you this?"

"I am no Jew," said Pilate, "Your own leaders have sent you to me. Now, what have you done?"

Jesus said, "My kingdom is not of this world. If it was, my servants would be fighting to keep me from the Jews."

"Then you are a king?" asked Pilate.

"As you say," said Jesus, "This is why I was born and why I came into this world, to testify to the truth. Whoever loves truth listens to my voice."

"What is truth?" said Pilate. He got up and went out to the crowd. "I find no guilt in him," he said, "But I know it is a custom on Passover to release one prisoner. Shall I release for you that so-called King of the Jews or shall I release the murderer Barabbas?"

At that moment, a messenger came to Pilate with a note from his wife that said, "Have nothing to do with that innocent man. I have had a terrible dream about him!"

The leaders stirred up the crowd and they shouted "Barabbas! Release Barabbas!"

"And what should I do with King of the Jews?" said Pilate.

"Crucify him!" they shouted, "Crucify him!"

Pilate, wanting nothing to do with Jesus said, "I find no guilt in him, but to satisfy you I will have him whipped."

The Romans took Jesus into the barracks where the soldiers lashed him with whips tipped with lead weights and with sharp pieces of bone. Then they wove a crown of thorns and pushed it onto his head. They put a fine kingly robe on him and placed a reed in his hand for a scepter and they made fun of him saying "Hail King of the Jews!" They punched him and plucked the reed from his hand and struck him with it.

When they had their fun, Pilate had him brought out, beaten and bloody, still wearing the crown of thorns and the robe. "Look at the man!" said Pilate, hoping that the crowd would be satisfied.

But they shouted "Crucify him! Crucify him!"

"I find no guilt in him, crucify him yourselves!" said Pilate, knowing that they could not.

"According to our laws, he must die because he claims to be the Son of God," said the priests. Now this frightened Pilate because the Son of God was a title the Romans gave only to Caesar, their own emperor.

Pilate had Jesus brought back into the barracks. "Where are you from?" he asked. Jesus said nothing. "You are not speaking to me?" asked Pilate, "Don't you know that I have the power to release you or to crucify you?"

Jesus said, "You would have no power over me if it had not been given you from above."

Pilate went to the crowd and said he would release Jesus but that made them furious. They said that if he released Jesus, he was no friend of Caesar. Pilate had Jesus brought out. "Look at your king!" he said.

"Take him away! Crucify him! Crucify him!" they said.

"What?" said Pilate, "Shall I crucify your king?"

"We have no king but Caesar," said the priests.

When Pilate saw that a riot was about to break out, he had water brought to him and he washed his hands in front of the crowd saying, "I am innocent of this man's blood. Do with him as you will." Then he had Barabbas released. Jesus was taken back into the barracks where they dressed him in his own clothes and handed him over to be crucified.

When Judas Iscariot heard that Jesus was condemned to death, he became very sorry for what he had done. He went to the priests in the temple and said, "I have sinned in betraying an innocent man."

"That is your problem," they said.

Judas took the thirty pieces of silver they had paid him and threw them on the temple floor. Then he went out and hanged himself.

The guards took Jesus and forced him to carry his cross through the streets of Jerusalem until they picked a man named Simon, from the country of Cyrene, and made him carry the cross behind Jesus since Jesus was weakened from his beatings. The people of the city were just now hearing that Jesus of Nazareth had been condemned to death. Large crowds came out and followed Jesus including many women who were mourning and crying over him.

He turned to them and said, "Daughters of Jerusalem, don't cry for me; but, for yourselves and your children, because the days are coming when people will say 'Blessed are the wombs that never gave birth and the breasts that never nursed.' In those days people will say to the mountains 'Fall on us!' and to the hills 'Cover us!' for if this evil is done when the wood is green, what will happen when it is dry?" (He was foretelling the destruction of Jerusalem which would be done by the Romans forty years later.)

They went outside the gates to a hill called The Place of the Skull, which in the language of those days was called Golgotha and in Latin was called Calvary. There the Roman soldiers nailed his hands and feet to the cross and lifted it up, so Jesus hung on it. They placed Jesus between two criminals who were also being crucified. As was customary, the crime of the condemned was written on a board placed on the cross over his head; it read "Jesus of Nazareth, King of the Jews."

After the soldiers had hung Jesus on the cross, they divided his clothes among themselves, but they did not want to cut up his cloak for it was expensive, so they threw dice for it. Then they sat and kept watch over him.

Jesus said from the cross, "Father, forgive them for they don't know what they are doing."

Some in the crowd, and some passing by, mocked him, shaking their heads and saying, "Save yourself if you are the Son of God!" and "Come down from the cross!" The chief priests and scribes and elders also mocked him saying "He saved others, but he can't save himself. He is the king of Israel? Let the Messiah, the King of Israel come down off the cross now and then we will believe him. He trusted God; let Him save him now if He wants. After all, he said 'I am the Son of God!"

One of the criminals hanging beside him also mocked him saying, "Aren't you the Messiah? Save yourself and us too." But the other said, "Have you no fear of God? We are guilty of our crimes, but this man has done nothing." Then he said, "Jesus, remember me when you come into your kingdom."

Jesus told him, "Today you will be with me in Paradise."

Standing by Jesus, witnessing his agony, were his mother and her sister, and Mary, the wife of Clopas, and Mary Magdalen, and John, the only one of the Twelve who had not deserted him. Seeing her son pierced, Mary's heart was pierced. When Jesus saw his mother and John together, he said to her "Woman, this is your son." And to John he said, "This is your mother." From that moment on, John cared for and provided for Mary as his own mother.

From noon until three in the afternoon, a darkness hung over the land. Then at about three Jesus cried out "My God, My God, why have you abandoned me?' recalling the words of the twenty-second Psalm which foretold of this very hour, and many in the crowd understood. He knew the end was near, so to fulfill prophesy, Jesus said "I thirst." They put a sponge on a pole and, soaking it in wine, they put it up to his mouth. When Jesus had taken some, he said "It is finished." Then he cried allowed, "Father into your hands I commend my spirit!" and he hung his head and died.

When he died the ground shook, rocks split, and tombs opened and those who came out of the tombs were seen by many in the city. And the huge curtain that hung across the width of the temple to separate the place of God from the place of men was torn in two from top to bottom. When the Roman officer who was there saw the earthquake and other wonders, he said "Truly this was the Son of God." Many people who had been there became afraid and were sorry they had done what they did. The women who had been following Jesus were standing nearby and saw all these things.

Sundown was approaching, and it was illegal for dead bodies to be unburied after dark. So, to hasten their deaths, the soldiers broke the legs of the two criminals, so their lungs would be pulled by their own body weight and they could not breathe. But when the soldiers came to Jesus, they found he was already dead. One of the soldiers thrust a spear into his side and out flowed blood and water. This fulfilled the ancient writing that said, "Not a bone of his will be broken" and "They will look upon him whom they pierced."

There was a rich man named Joseph of Arimathea who was a member of the Sanhedrin but was not part of their plot to kill Jesus. In fact, he was a secret follower of Jesus. He bravely went to Pilate to ask for the body of Jesus. Pilate permitted it so Joseph had Jesus taken down and wrapped in a clean cloth. The tomb that Joseph had cut for himself was nearby, so they placed Jesus in that tomb and rolled the heavy stone across the entrance. Then they disbursed, but Mary of Magdala and many of the women stayed sitting there, facing the tomb. Finally, they left so as not be out at night.

The Jews placed guards at the tomb to prevent his followers from taking the body and faking his resurrection. So, outside the tomb, a few soldiers tried to keep warm on their lonely vigil while the body of Jesus lay in the pitch dark of the stone-cold tomb, for he was dead.

166

# 7

# I Have Seen the Lord

## The New Beginning

*The Lord says to my lord, "Take your throne at my right hand; I make your enemies your footstool. Your mighty scepter will extend out from Jerusalem. Rule over your enemies. Yours is power from the day of your birth. Before the sun existed, I begot you like the dew. You are a priest forever according to the order of Melchizedek."*

*Psalm 110*

## The Empty Tomb
From the Good News According to Mark and John

At early dawn on the day after the Sabbath, there was another earthquake and an angel of the Lord came down and rolled the stone aside. His appearance was like lightning. The guards fainted in fear. When they awoke, they ran to the priests to tell them what had happened. The priests bribed them and ordered them not to repeat what they had said.

That same morning, Mary of Magdala and two of the other women took up the spices they had prepared and went out toward the tomb in the hope of properly cleaning and anointing the body of Jesus since he was buried in a hurry. They talked among themselves, wondering who would roll back the heavy stone for them. When they arrived, they found the stone had been rolled away and saw that the tomb was empty. They ran back to tell

167

The Rock and the others who were grieving. When Mary told them the tomb was empty, The Rock and John ran out to the tomb. John arrived first and stopped at the entrance. The Rock caught up and went into the tomb, then John followed him in. They saw the cloth which had wrapped Jesus. Lying separately was the neatly rolled cloth that covered his face. They did not understand what had happened and they returned home in grief.

But Mary of Magdala, and some of the women, remained at the tomb, crying uncontrollably. As she was crying, Mary looked in the tomb and saw two men dressed in white.

"Woman, why are you crying?" said one.

"They have taken my Lord," she said, "and I don't know where he is."

"Why do you seek the living among the dead?" the man said. "He is not here but he has been raised. Remember what he said to you in Galilee; that the Son of Man must be crucified by sinners and will rise on the third day."

Mary was confused. She turned and saw a man standing nearby. "Woman," he said, "Why are you crying? Who are you looking for?"

She thought it was the gardener and she said, "Sir, if you took him away please tell me and I will come and take him."

"Mary." he said.

At that she saw that it was Jesus. "Teacher!" she cried. And she fell at his feet and hugged his knees and the other women did also.

"You must let me go," said Jesus, "For I have not yet ascended to my Father. Go back to my brothers and tell them I am going to my Father and your Father, to my God and your God."

They ran back in great joy. Mary went to The Rock and the others saying, "I have seen The Lord!" And she told them all that had happened.

## On the Road to Emmaus
From the Good News According to Luke

Later that day, two of the men who had been with them left Jerusalem and headed for the town of Emmaus which was not very far away. They were not convinced that Mary had really seen Jesus and they began to talk about it as they walked. They met a man on the road who started walking with them.

"What are you talking about?" he said.

They stopped, and one said, 'Are you the only visitor to Jerusalem who does not know the things that have been happening these past days?"

"What things?" said the man.

"About Jesus of Nazareth," they said. "He was a great and mighty prophet who worked many miracles. The chief priests had him crucified. We were hoping that he was The Messiah. Some of our women went to his tomb this morning and said they had a vision that angels told them he is alive but some of our men went out and did not see him."

"Oh, how foolishly slow you are to believe the prophets," said the man. "Wasn't it necessary for the Messiah to suffer in order to enter into his glory?" Then he walked with them and, beginning with Moses and all the prophets, he showed them how their writings foretold all the very things that had happened to Jesus.

When they got to Emmaus, they asked the man to stay with them a while. When they sat to eat, the man took the bread, broke it, said a blessing, and passed it to them. At that, they saw that the man was Jesus, but as soon as they recognized him, he vanished.

The men said to each other, "Weren't our hearts burning within us as he spoke to us on the road and explained the sacred writings to us?" Then they got up and hurried back to Jerusalem to tell the others what had happened.

## Jesus Appears to Thomas
From the Good News According to John and Matthew

In Jerusalem, the Rock and the others were in one room in a house which was locked because they were afraid that the Jews would come and arrest them.

Jesus appeared standing before them and said, "Peace be with you."

They were terrified, thinking they were seeing a ghost.

"Why are you afraid?" said Jesus. "Look. See my hands and my feet. Touch me so you may know that I am flesh and bones and no ghost."

While they were still amazed, he asked them if they had anything to eat. Someone produced a piece of baked fish which he took and ate. Then he said, "While I was still with you, I told you that these things would happen as they were foretold by Moses and the Prophets and the Psalms. The Messiah would suffer and rise from the dead on the third day and that redemption from sins would be preached to the whole world beginning with Jerusalem."

Then he said to them, "Peace be with you. As the Father has sent me, so I send you." Then he breathed on them saying, "Receive the Holy Spirit. Whose sins you forgive are forgiven and whose sins you retain are retained."

Now, Thomas, one of The Twelve, was not present at that time. When the others told him that Jesus had appeared to them, he would not believe it saying, "Unless I put my fingers in the nail holes and place my hand in the hole in his side, I will not believe it."

About a week later, they were all in one room again and Thomas was with them. Then, although the doors were locked, Jesus appeared before them again saying, "Peace be with you." Then he said to Thomas, "Put your finger here in my hand and place your hand here in my side and believe."

Thomas did so and said, "My Lord and my God."

Jesus said, "You believe because you have seen. Blessed are those who believe and have not seen."

Over the next forty days Jesus appeared many times before many people and, all together, five hundred people saw him alive after his resurrection. On one occasion, The Eleven had gathered on a hilltop in Galilee where Jesus had told them to assemble. He came to them and said, "All power in Heaven and Earth has been given to me. So, you go out and make followers in all nations, baptizing them in the name of the Father, and of the Son, and of the Holy Spirit, teaching them to observe all that I have commanded you, and I will be with you until the end of time."

## Jesus and The Rock
From the Good News According to John

One morning during those forty days, before dawn, Simon, who is The Rock, and Thomas, and James and John, and two others of The Eleven were in a boat fishing on the Sea of Galilee. When dawn broke, they saw a man standing on the shore.

He called to them "Children, have you caught anything to eat?" They said no, so he said, "Cast your net over the other side of the boat and you will catch something."

They cast out the net and it filled with so many fish that they couldn't haul it in. Realizing that it must be Jesus, Simon jumped into the water and swam to shore while the others rowed onto the shore, pulling the net behind the boat. They found Jesus and the Rock waiting with a fire with cooked fish and bread. He handed them some bread and fish and they ate.

After they had eaten, Jesus said to the Rock, "Simon, son of Jonah, do you love me?"

The Rock said, "Yes Lord, you know I do."

Jesus said, "Feed my lambs." Again, he said, "Simon, so of Jonah, do you love me?'

The Rock said, "Yes Lord, you know I love you."

Jesus said, "Tend my flock." Again, he said, "Simon son of Jonah, do you love me?"

The Rock became perturbed and said, "Lord, you know everything. You know I love you."

Jesus said, "Feed my sheep.

"Simon, when you were young you used to dress yourself and go where you wanted; but when you are older, you will stretch out your hands and someone else will dress you and lead you to where you don't want to go. As I have done." This was a reference to Simon The Rock's future cruci-fixion. And Jesus said to him, "Follow me."

## The Ascension of Jesus
From the Book of the Acts of the Apostles

One day he led them to Bethany on the Mount of Olives, not far from the garden in which he was arrested.

One of them asked, "Lord, are you now going to restore the kingdom of Israel?"

He said, "It is not for you to know the things that the Father has established and ordained. But you will receive power when the Holy Spirit comes upon you, and you will be my ambassadors throughout Judea and Samaria, and to the ends of the Earth."

Then he raised his hands as a blessing over them and, as they watched, he was lifted up into the air, and taken to the sky in a cloud, and they did not see him again.

As they were looking up, suddenly two men dressed in white were standing among them. They said, "Men of Galilee, why are you standing there looking up at the sky? This Jesus who has been taken up from you into Heaven will return in the same way as you saw him go."

Then they returned to Jerusalem and were constantly at prayer in the temple. And great things were about to happen.

# BOOK III
## THE HOLY SPIRIT

# Revelation

The divine or supernatural disclosure to humans of something relating to
human existence or the world.

Book Three communicates the commentaries of the earliest Christian writers through a series of dialogues that take place between John, the last of
the Apostles, and Laurentius, the governor of Patmos, the island to where
John was exiled, and where he wrote the last book of the Bible. It is topical and its structure mirrors The Apostles' Creed which is a still popular
capsule of Christian thought that pre-dates the Bible. The dialogues are
hypothetical, but John's words are Biblical. Though not mentioned in the
Bible, the people, places, and events in Book Three were borrowed from
Church history to provide a framework for the dialogues, and to personalize the teachings therein for the reader.

# 1

# Do You Understand What You Are Reading?

## *Memories*

### From the Acts of the Apostles

*May God be gracious to us and bless us. May His face shine upon us. May His rule be known upon the Earth and His saving power among all the nations. May all the peoples of the Earth praise you, God. May the nations be glad and shout with joy for your governance is just. May the peoples praise you, Lord; may all the peoples praise you!*

*Psalm 67*

It was a cool, clear, promising morning. Laurentius rose quietly, draped his tunic over his shoulders and smiled down at Chrysippe; she was still asleep. He looked up through the window and saw vivid blue. Summers can be sweltering, and winters can be stormy but spring in the Aegean was magnificent. Today, the rocky hills will be covered with vibrant wildflowers. The sea will send a gentle breeze to temper the warm sun as he drives Chrysippe and the children, reining the horse himself, over the hill and down to the only sandy beach on the island. If the gods please, they will be alone; no servants, no guards, no petitioners. He and Chrysippe will revel in the frolics of their children. They will lunch on a blanket in the shade of the rocks and, as the day warms, the children will play in the surf. He may just join them.

Laurentius had been eager for this day. He thought his assignment would be a quiet one. How much trouble can be had on an island that one could walk end to end in half a day? But trouble there was. Was it here before, or had it followed him from Ephesus? How can so few people want so much and be unhappy with what they have? But that would be tolerable if not for Apollonides. During his seizure, the other day he pounded his head till it bled and then he broke the nose of the servant who tried to help him. How many more before he kills himself or someone else? How Chrysippe cries, wondering if her beloved brother will be a lunatic for the rest of his life.

"Today is for our own little family, and for the beach," thought Laurentius, "Just today for us." He dressed and started to go to see to the arrangements for the outing. He opened the bedroom door and standing there, waiting, was the head servant.

"Master" he said, "He is back."

"Apollonides?" said Laurentius.

"No" said the servant, "The other one."

"Oh no," said Laurentius. His shoulders dropped, part in relief that it was not his mad brother-in-law, and part in resignation. He could not avoid the other one any longer.

"He is at the gate," said the servant, "He arrived after sunset and has been sitting there all night, in the cold."

Laurentius grit his teeth. He squared himself and walked out through the shady atrium to the front gate and out to the street. There, on the curb, was a slightly built man with a gray beard and a face like flint. He stood when he saw Laurentius and straightened himself to his fullest height which was almost as straight as a younger man.

"John, you old fool!" said Laurentius, "Why are you here again?"

"You know why I am here, Governor!" answered the man, "It is the same reason why I was here yesterday."

"And the day before, and the day before that," said Laurentius.

"If you had come out and seen me then, I would not have to be here now," said John. "If you had seen me in the government building, I would not have to come to your house."

"I saw you a week ago in the government building," said Laurentius, "and I answered your petition."

"It was the wrong answer." said John.

"You are a fox!" said Laurentius, "You try to embarrass me in front of my neighbors so all will see that the governor of Patmos will not aid a poor crazy old man. But you are also a fool. If they knew your petition, they would not be so sympathetic toward you. You are an exile, a prisoner here, and you are allowed to walk about only by my good graces. Do you not know that I have the power of life and death over you, you old Jew?"

"You would have no power if it had not been given to you from above," said John, "and you know I have much sympathy on this island, even within your own family, so you cannot silence me or make me disappear with no consequences."

A few people had stopped to listen as best they could from across the street. Laurentius took a breath and lowered his voice. "Why, John, did you just not go ahead and do it without asking me?"

"Because you are the governor," answered the old man in a lowered voice, "and I do my best to obey the law."

"If you had done better, you wouldn't be in exile here," said Laurentius. "Be that as it may, I know people love you here. I will hear you again; but not today! Come to the basilica tomorrow, at the end of the workday."

"Done," said John, and he walked away.

The shadows had lengthened while Laurentius waited on the steps of the government building. He had considered going home at the usual time but, if John said he would be there, he would be there; and the last thing he wanted was for John to come looking for him at his house again. So, he waited.

Before long, the familiar form crossed the plaza, climbed the steps and sat beside him.

"How was your outing?" asked John.

"Good."

"Thank you for seeing me again."

"Did I have a choice?"

"We all have choices," said John.

"What is it, then, about you?" said Laurentius. "You are an intelligent man. You could have lived a good life, yet you chose a life of poverty and rejection. Most of you followers of Jesus are like rabbits, they stay still and quiet and go unnoticed and they live their lives in peace. But others, like you, go out into the field in the middle of the day, and the eagle swoops.

"Your man, Paul; I was a youth when he caused a riot in Ephesus; publicly insulting the gods of Rome. How lucky he was to survive. But the Roman eagle did finally snatch him up and now he is dead. Your Rock also, crucified upside down."

"And Stephen," said John. "One of the first to be ordained by us to be a servant of the Assembly, stoned by the Jews for proclaiming the truth of Jesus the Messiah. And my own brother, James, put to death by the sword on the orders of Herod. How I have missed him."

"But you," said Laurentius, "lucky enough to be exiled and spared the grizzly executions that so many of you underwent. Why don't you just lay low and live your life? What drives you?"

"The Holy Spirit," said John.

"And what is the Holy Spirit?" asked Laurentius.

"Not a 'what,'" said John, "a 'who'."

"You mean a god?" asked Laurentius.

John pondered a moment then said, "It was very long ago. My beard was not yet full, but I had followed Jesus for three years and seen many wonderful things. After he rose from the dead and ascended back into Heaven, we established our Assembly in Jerusalem. There was a feast of the Jews and many pilgrims were gathered in the city. I was with The Rock, and my brother James, and several others. We were in one room together when, suddenly, a great noise, like a mighty wind, filled the room. I was terrified. Then there appeared to us things like tongues of fire that separated and multiplied before us and came to rest on each of us. We were filled with the Holy Spirit and were in ecstasy.

"There were many Jews about, from all different parts of the world, since it was the time of a major celebration for the Jews. When they heard the noise, they came to see what had happened and they found us proclaiming the good news of Jesus Christ, as bold as drunken men."

"Unusual," said Laurentius.

"There's more," said John. "These people, though Jews, were from many different countries: from Parthia, from Egypt, from Rome. There were Medes and Arabs, Cretans, and Phrygians, and so many others. And each of them heard us speak in their own language! Though we did not know those languages! Everyone was astounded.

"Then, The Rock stepped forward and proclaimed to them how this event fulfilled prophesy and he explained to them, in the most elegant terms, how Jesus, whom some of them had crucified, is the Messiah. He quoted scripture and used reason and was persuasive in a way he could have never been before that moment.

"That day three thousand people were baptized and added to our numbers. After the celebration, they carried the Good News of Jesus to their homes all around the world.

"Since then we were no longer afraid. We knew what to do and we knew that the Holy Spirit, which Jesus had promised us, was now with us and there was nothing that was going to stop the spreading of the Kingdom of God."

"So," said Laurentius, "you are a party to miracles. They say you arrived in a miracle. Before I even saw you the crew of the ship that brought you here told me how a young man was washed overboard and how you prayed, and a wave washed him right back on the ship. They think that was a miracle; but I think it was luck and the boy would have survived if you prayed or not."

"You do not believe in miracles?" said John.

"I believe in coincidences," said Laurentius.

"Do you believe in the gods?" asked John.

"I believe in what the State says I should believe in," answered Laurentius. "But," he said after a pause, "the philosophers encourage us to have open minds; so, what is it like to be a part of a miracle?"

After another pause John spoke. "One day, in those early days,

The Rock and I were walking into the temple in Jerusalem and we came upon a crippled beggar. He asked for alms. The Rock said 'Look at us. I have no silver or gold, but what I do have I give you in the name of Jesus of Nazareth, the Messiah. Stand and walk.' The Rock took the man by the hand and raised him up and the man walked and began jumping and praising God. Many people knew he was a cripple and they were amazed. A crowd gathered, and The Rock spoke to them of Jesus.

"We gained such a reputation that people would place their sick and crippled on the ground at the entrance to the temple so our shadows would pass over them and they would be cured; and we would speak of Jesus. All the many signs and wonders I have seen and done were followed by expositions of the Good News of Jesus Christ. The true miracles were not just in the signs and wonders, but in the conversions of the hearts of those who listened.

"And for many, no signs were needed, and they were converted through their intellect. One day Phillip, one of the Twelve, was on the road to Gaza when he came upon an Ethiopian official on his way home from Jerusalem. He was in his chariot reading from the prophet Isaiah. Phillip asked him 'Do you understand what you are reading?' The official said, 'How can I unless someone explains it to me?' so Phillip explained how the prophecy was about Jesus and the official understood and was baptized by Phillip that day.

"Maybe you will be like the Ethiopian official."

"Not likely," said Laurentius.

John looked out at the lengthening shadows that had crept over the plaza. He said, "We lived in Jerusalem for a while; the wealthy among us sharing with the less fortunate. Our numbers grew. We attracted the attention of the Sanhedrin; the council of elders, the same who had Jesus crucified. They ordered us to stop talking about Jesus, but we continued. That's when they stoned Stephen.

"But the Lord was with us. We made converts throughout Judea and Samaria. The Rock converted a Roman official named Cornelius. He baptized Cornelius and his entire household.

"For a while we were at peace and we prospered. We appointed and ordained overseers to rule the local assemblies and ordained elders and servers to assist us since our numbers had grown so.

"But this was not to last. Herod, the one who was prince when Jesus was crucified, began to persecute us. Many were arrested. That's when James was executed.

"The Rock was imprisoned during those times." John said with a faint smile. "The night before his trial, the Rock was in prison; double chained, sleeping between two soldiers in a locked cell while other soldiers stood guard outside. Then he was awakened by someone tapping on him. It was an angel bathed in light. 'Get up,' the angel said, and the Rock's chains just fell off him. The angel said, 'put on your cloak and follow me." The Rock did so, thinking he was having a vision. They walked out of the cell and through the anteroom to the iron gate which led out to the city. It opened by itself. They went out and the angel disappeared. The Rock, realizing it was truly happening, made his way to a house where several of us were staying. He knocked on the outer door and a servant girl answered it. She was so excited that she ran inside to tell the others but didn't open the door. We all thought she was crazy, but the Rock kept knocking and we opened the door and saw him. He stayed with us just a short time and then left the city. Herod had the whole city searched; but did not find him.

"We went out after that. We traveled alone, in pairs, in groups; all over the world. We preached the Good News of Jesus to all who would listen. We founded and built up assemblies in so many cities and towns. Once we had trained up a good man in an assembly, we ordained him as the overseer, and entrusted him to shepherd the people. Then we moved on and did it again. And, as far as I know, I am the last of that first generation."

"Tell me of Paul," said Laurentius, "He's the one I saw myself in Ephesus. I was young, but I remember him to be an average looking man but so determined; so brave, and yet so stupid. No, not stupid. Misguided. He stirred up trouble where there was no trouble to be seen and brought wrath upon himself."

"Paul," said John, "Paul had been a temple official, a Pharisee. He was against us. Through his actions, many of the Christians were arrested and imprisoned or executed by the Jews. He traveled around, warrants in hand, and arrested Christians all around Judea and the surrounding lands.

"One day he was traveling to Damascus to arrest Christians. As he neared the city a blinding light from heaven flashed before him and he fell to the ground. He heard a voice saying, 'Paul, why do you persecute me?' 'Who are you?' asked Paul. And the voice said, 'I am Jesus whom you are persecuting. Get up, go into the city and you will be told what to do.' The men who were with Paul were astounded, for they too heard the voice, though they did not see the light. When Paul opened his eyes, he was blind. His companions led him to the city where he remained blind for three days and ate or drank nothing.

"Now, there was one of our number in Damascus. His name was Ananias. The Lord came to him in a vision and told him where to find Paul. Ananias knew that Paul was a great enemy of the Christians, but the Lord revealed to him that he would use Paul for His own glory. So, Ananias went to where Paul was. He said, 'My brother Paul, The Lord Jesus, who appeared to you on the road, has sent me to you that you may see and be filled with the Holy Spirit.' Then things like scales fell from Paul's eyes and he could see. He was baptized. He ate and drank and regained his strength and went to stay with some believers.

"He stayed in Damascus and, after some time, he gained the trust of the Christians and he preached and debated with the Jews, confounding their logic. The Jews in Damascus conspired to kill him. He got news of their plot and, one night, had himself lowered over the wall in a basket and he made his escape. He went to Jerusalem; this was when we were still to-gether there. We avoided him, but Barnabas took him under his wing, and we came to trust him. He spent time with us, conversing with The Rock and going out to debate Jews and Greeks alike. We had heard that the Jews in Jerusalem had planned to kill him, so we took him to Caesarea and put him on a ship to Tarsus, which was his hometown.

"After that, he was unstoppable; traveling for years throughout Asia Minor and Greece, preaching, debating, working miracles, and winning converts. By then he was one of us; an ambassador of the Assembly of Jesus. He founded many local assemblies and ordained several overseers and elders. It was during these times that he was in Ephesus where you saw him."

"Yes," said Laurentius. "There was a great crowd of angry men marching down the street shouting 'Great is Artemis! Great is Ephesus!' Well, I was young, I wanted to see the excitement. The crowd flowed into the theater. You could hear their shouts echoing in the streets. I tried to get in, but I couldn't push past the crowd. There was a group of men in the street arguing. I went to see. One man was saying 'I must go in there to explain!' And the others were holding him back saying 'no, Paul, the crowd will tear you apart!' He kept pushing forward, but they kept pushing back and he could not advance. Then I saw an opening at the theater entrance, so I rushed in and men were shouting and running around to and fro. Many were saying 'What's going on? What are we here for?' It was marvelous pandemonium. After some time, the city clerk gained the attention and said something like 'If you have something against these men, take them to court, but if you do not disburse, you could all be arrested for rioting!' Well this calmed them down and the whole thing fizzled out. I later heard that it was Paul's fault though I never found out why."

"I can enlighten you," said John. "The silversmiths in the city became worried, since Paul was converting so many people away from the worship of the goddess Artemis, that they would lose their livelihoods, which was making statues of Artemis. So, they worked up the people against the preachers of the new religion. Paul had to leave Ephesus after that.

"Now," he said, "It is late. The sun has almost set, and I must go back to my cave while there is still light. What do say? Do I have your yes?"

"No," said Laurentius, "It would not be wise."

John took a deep breath. "You are a stubborn young man," he said.

"I am a cautious and pragmatic man," said Laurentius. "That is how I became an accomplished bureaucrat. And it is how I will keep my job."

"Well," said John as he pushed himself up from the steps, "You are tired. I'm sure you want to see your family. We will talk later."

"There is no need for further talk," said Laurentius.

"It is a small island." said John as he walked away, "We will see each other. Good night."

# 2

# The Visible of the Invisible God

## *On God*

From the letters entitled Acts, Romans, 1st and 2nd Corinthians, Galatians, Ephesians, Philippians, Colossians, Hebrews, 2nd Timothy, and 1st John.

*God's word is true; all His works are trustworthy. The Lord loves justice and fills the Earth with goodness. By His word, the heavens were made, and waters of the sea gathered as in a bowl. Let all the Earth love the Lord and all who dwell in it revere Him. For He spoke, and it came to be; commanded and it was set. The plans of man are foiled and frustrated, but the plan of God stands forever; wise designs through all generations.*

*Psalm 33*

The next day Laurentius walked home for lunch since there was no pressing business. He found Chrysippe alone at her loom. He did not marry her for her beauty, but beautiful she was, despite childbirth and family cares. When she looked up and saw him, a scowl fell over her face.

"What's wrong?" asked Laurentius, "Is it your brother? What has he done? Is he alright?"

"It is not Apollonides," she said.

"Then what?"

"You told John he couldn't send his letter," she announced.

"Was that all?' he thought. "How did you know? Who told you, your father?"

"Never mind how I know. John is a nice old man and he would not harm anyone. Let him do as he wishes."

"My Dear," said Laurentius, "this is business of state, not family."

"My father adores him. And for that matter, so do I. That makes it family business. And so, the business of John is my business."

"If your father adores him so, why did he kick him out of his home to live in a cave?"

"That was John's choice," she said, "I don't know why, but he visits Father every morning and people assemble there to worship the One God."

She lowered her head slightly and approached him.

"Here it comes," he thought.

"Darling," she said as she put her arms around his neck, "talk to him again. See what you can do."

He sighed. He could command her, he could chastise her, he could beat her if she needed it; but he had no defense against this, and they both knew it. "Have him come by the government building after work hours," he said.

It was a repeat of the previous day. Laurentius, sitting on the steps, watched John approach.

"How can it be," said Laurentius, "that and old foreign exile has such influence in my little governorship?"

"Perhaps it is a miracle," said John as he eased himself onto the steps next to Laurentius.

"The work of the One True God, no doubt," said Laurentius. "How one god can do so many things, is beyond me. You know, the gods of Olympus share power; Zeus the sky, Poseidon the water; Hera the house-hold; Artemis, the woods, and so on. How can one God do everything?"

"When Paul was at Athens," said John, 'he saw many shrines to the various gods. One, he saw, was dedicated to an unknown god. This he pro-claimed to be the One God who made everything. God does not dwell in sanctuaries or in shrines nor does He need offerings for He needs nothing.

Rather He gives all things. From one man he made all of mankind to dwell on the Earth and he ordered the natural world so that man may seek him and find him. For he is not far away like the gods of Olympus. In fact, we are in him and from him as his children. And those who are baptized are made children of God by adoption through His Holy Spirit."

Laurentius pondered a moment then said, "Our gods were all born or created from long ago and, I suppose, like their predecessors, the Titans, they will be succeeded some day; they will end. Who created your god, how will he end?"

"He is eternal," said John.

"No beginning and no end," said Laurentius. "Some of our greatest philosophers have put forth such a theory; that since everything is created by something that came before it, and since nothing can create itself, it must all have begun with one thing that was un-created, and therefore, always was."

"Every house was begun by someone but the beginner of all is God," said the old man.

"And your Jesus is his oracle?" asked Laurentius.

"There is one God," said John, "from whom all things are, and one Lord, Jesus Christ, through whom all things are. In the past, God spoke to us through prophets. In these days, he has spoken to us through His Son, who is the visible of the invisible God, the light of God, the exact imprint of His being. The fullness of God is in Him. In Him all things were created, whether in Heaven or on Earth, visible and invisible. He is before all things and he sustains all things by his powerful word."

"Jesus was before all things," said Laurentius, "and all things were created through him. Yet he was a man born of woman. How could he exist before he was born?"

John answered, saying "Though he was of the substance of God, he emptied himself and made himself lowly, to be a man. In the fullness of time, he made himself to be born of a virgin. Though he was crowned with glory, for a little while he was a man, lower than the angels, so to call us brothers. Since he shared in our flesh and blood, he could taste death and so destroy the one who has the power of death, Satan, and free those who, through fear of death, have been slaves all their lives. Because Jesus, the sinless, died for us sinners to reconcile us with God through his death on a cross."

"This is the sacrifice you Christians speak of, is it not?" said Laurentius. "We too offer sacrifices to our gods. I think most religions do in one way or another. We give treasure to oracles or offer up animals to the gods. Your Jews did the same thing before the Romans destroyed their temple. I know they killed lambs or bulls, offering the blood of animals as a substitute for their own blood; because they knew they themselves were sinners and deserving of death for their offenses. But their god, in his mercy accepted the blood of the sacrificed animals as payment. And since they sinned over and over, they had to offer sacrifices over and over. This is not unlike our religion, and most others. It is ironic, though, how the same generation witnessed the death of Jesus was the last generation to offer sacrifices in their temple."

"Yes." said John, "In the Jewish tradition, the priests often offered sacrifices for certain people or certain reasons, but once a year, the high priest entered the Holy of Holies in the temple of Jerusalem and offered the blood of the victims as payment for his sins and of all the people. When Jesus came as high priest, he offered a sacrifice once and for all; not with the blood of animals, but with his own blood, thus gaining for us eternal payment, that is, eternal redemption from our sins. For if the blood of animals can cleanse the sinner, how much more will the blood of Jesus Christ, who freely offered himself as a victim for us, cleanse our souls so that we may grow closer to God? And so, through the mediation of Jesus, we are children of God and no more sacrifices are needed."

Laurentius was quiet for some time. "This is powerful," he said. "We have stories in our religion of gods who make themselves to appear like men, but it is for their own pleasure. To think that a god, The God, would make himself man just to be his own sacrificial victim and die; to die for us; this is powerful."

John said, "After he died for our sins he was buried. In spirit he went to preach to the faithful dead. Then, on the third day, he rose from the dead in fulfillment of the prophesies. He appeared to the Rock, then to the Eleven, and later, to five hundred people at one time. After forty days, he ascended into Heaven and now his name is above every name, that at the name of Jesus, every knee shall bend, in Heaven and on earth, and under the earth, and every mouth confess that Jesus Christ is Lord.

"On the last day Jesus will return, descending from heaven with a cry of command, with the voice of power, and with the sound of the trumpet of God. And the dead will rise and appear before the judgment seat of Jesus Christ, so that each may receive his reward according to what he has done on earth, whether good or evil."

Laurentius pondered again. "I am a man of reason," he said, "a natural man. I believe what I see, and I doubt what I don't see. How can I judge the truth of what you say? You are a witness, I know. There were many witnesses, I know. But how does one know the mind of God?"

John looked deeply at Laurentius, "A natural person does not know the Spirit of God. So, to a natural person this is foolishness. Among us humans, no one knows what is in a man's heart, but his own spirit knows. Similarly, no one knows the mind of God except the Holy Spirit of God. In that room on that day we received the Holy Spirit of God, as Jesus had promised, so that we may understand the spiritual truths that God has given to us. And this Spirit comes to our aid in our weakness and intercedes on our behalf. This Holy Spirit of God produces talents and gifts in us and moves us to use them to the glory of God."

Again, Laurentius was silent for some time. "So," he said, almost to himself, "there is one God who has no beginning and no end, and who needs nothing because he is the source of everything. And there is Father, and Son, and Holy Spirit; all of God. I thought I knew something of the Jewish faith, but this is foreign to me. No one has explained this to me like you have. And this God, unlike all the gods I know, cares not for his own pleasure, since he needs nothing, but takes pleasure in caring for mortals, all mortals. There is something in this that satisfies both religion and philosophy. This is disturbing.

"John, I will think on this. Come back at the same time tomorrow." He got up and walked away.

Laurentius looked in on his children. Both asleep already. In the lamp light he studied their placid faces. If God is the father of the Christians, would he not love the Christians as he himself loves his own two children? Wouldn't a father who is God love more than a father who is man? How does a good father love? His own children were his joy, but they did get in the way sometimes. That was because there were other things, important things, to be done and because there was never enough time to do them. But what of a father who had all the time there is? Would his children ever bother him?

"The Christians gather at your father's house," said Laurentius to Chrysippe as she sat before the mirror undoing her hair."

She did not reply.

"Have you attended?" he asked.

"Did you talk to John today about his letter?" She replied.

"I did not," he said as he slipped under the covers. "It did not come up. We spoke of other things."

"What other things?"

"Very weighty things," he said. "Now, do you attend their gatherings?"

"I have attended," she answered.

"You must have heard John's preaching," he asked, "what do you think?"

"They are weighty things," she said. "Some are too weighty for me. But my father loves him, and I love my father."

"But I am your husband," he said.

She slipped under the covers next to him. "Are you going to forbid me from attending?"

"No," he said. "There is no law against it, and no real scandal, not here, not yet.

"How is your brother?"

"He had a good day today," she said, "nothing happened."

"Good then," he said as he patted her thigh. "Extinguish the lamp and sleep. All is well."

He rolled over, but he did not sleep.

# 3

# The Pillar and Foundation of Truth

## *On the Church*

From the letters entitled Acts, Romans, 1st Corinthians, Ephesians, Colossians, 1st Timothy, Titus, 1st Peter, and 2nd Peter.

*Happy those whose god is the Lord, the people chosen as His very own. From Heaven He looks down and sees all mankind, surveying from the royal throne all those on Earth. The One who fashioned the hearts of them all knows all they do. A king is not saved by armies nor a warrior delivered by strength, but the Lord's eyes are upon those who hope for His gracious deliverance. Our soul waits for the Lord who is our help and our shield. For in God our hearts rejoice; in His holy name we trust.*

*Psalm 33*

The old man was late. Laurentius had been sitting on the steps for a half hour. The governor loitering on public steps is an invitation for all to have a word or two. But now there was a lull. Most people were home or on their way home or somewhere eating supper.

John appeared from the direction which Laurentius expected. He walked wearily over and, giving a sigh, lowered himself onto the steps.

"You are late," said Laurentius.

190

"My apologies," said John, "some days it's hard for an old man to hike from his cave in the hills down to the center of town."

"Was it not your own choice to leave the comfort of my father-in-law's house?"

"I needed the solitude," said John, "to write my letter; the one which you have not yet given me permission to send."

"John," said Laurentius, "I have noticed a change in my father-in-law since you baptized him. He's been happier, less bothered. If you were to baptize my brother-in-law, Apollonides, do you think he too would be more content?"

"You love him, don't you?' said John.

"He was a youth when I married my wife," answered Laurentius. "I was a dashing officer, he idolized me, and I took him under my wing. For a while we were almost inseparable. But time marches on. I became a busy official and he is grown now. His eyes are no longer full of life. He is moody and angry, and no one knows why."

"I have not seen him lately," said John. "I was busy with my letter. It was written to seven assemblies in Asia."

"Seven?" said Laurentius. "Why seven? Can they not take care of themselves? Don't they have their own leaders? Why do you concern yourself with assemblies that you do not belong to?"

"We are many," John said, "and as one body has many members, so we who are many, are one body in Christ and, though individuals, we are members of one another. Just as the body is one but has many members, yet all are parts of the one body, so are we in Christ. If one member suffers, we all suffer, so we all care for one another. We are one body and one spirit with one hope, one Lord, one faith, one baptism, with one God and Father of all who is over all and through all and in all."

"So then, are you saying you are parts of your God?" asked Laurentius. "Are you holy like God? I don't think so. I have seen Christians make bad choices, and I have seen some Christians acting outside of the bounds of the love you profess."

"There are quarrels among us," said John, "and weakness, and sin. Even so we are all being fitted together into a dwelling place for God. God was in Christ, reconciling the world to himself, not counting our sins, but giving us reconciliation. So, by the holiness of Christ, we are a chosen people, a royal priesthood, a holy nation, God's own possession. And we proclaim the excellence of Him who has called us from darkness into light and shown us mercy."

"A new people then," said Laurentius. "But how is that? You are a Jew, yet you initiate Greeks. Will you start a nation from out of the Empire? Where will it be? Some say you Christians talk of rebellion and this is one reason why the Romans suspect you. Are their suspicions justified?"

John shook his head. "We accept subjugation to the governing authorities; for it is God's will that they rule. Because of this we pay taxes and we honor those to whom honor is due. We are neither Greek nor Jew, slave nor free, for God desires that all be saved and come to the knowledge of the truth."

"So" said Laurentius, "you are an egalitarian group? Have you no organization, no leaders? If not, then why should people read your letter?"

"Jesus Christ," said John, 'is the cornerstone of God's Assembly which he built on Simon, who is The Rock, and on the foundation of the Twelve, of whom I am the last. We were eyewitness of his majesty and, through the Holy Spirit, we have the prophetic word, the word of God made certain in our lifetime. All authority has been given to us."

"Certainly, you mean religious authority," said Laurentius, "since you, being a poor old exile, have no civil authority. Say, then, I grant that you have this authority; when you die, you being the last, does this authority die with you?"

John shook his head. "When the first of The Twelve, Judas, killed himself, we ordained another to take his office. His name was Matthias. As we went from place to place, founding local assemblies, we ordained good and trustworthy men to oversee them and we also appointed elders, or priest, in each assembly as well, and we authorized the overseers to also ordain good and faithful elders."

"Why this orderly succession?" asked Laurentius. "Now you sound like a government. Can't your Holy Spirit call a man to be an overseer apart from your government? Your Jews have holy scriptures; if your Holy

Spirit is with a man, should not his personal interpretation of those be valid apart from your organization?"

"There is no prophesy of scripture that is a matter of personal interpretation," said John, "for no prophesy was ever made just because a man wanted to be a prophet. There are those who are ignorant and unstable who twist the scriptures to their own destruction. It is we who have the prophetic word; people would do well to attend it like a lamp shining in a dark place.

"As for the idea of speaking for God apart from our 'government' as you call it; this has been tried. While we were still together in Jerusalem, men went out from among us without our sanction. They told the Greeks that, before they could become Christians, they first had to be circumcised like Jews. This caused much trouble among new converts and those considering conversion. Because of this, a delegation was sent to us in Jerusalem to ask us to settle the issue. We sent them back with a letter clearly stating that those who taught without our sanction were wrong. We stated that it was not simply our decision, but it was the decision of the Holy Spirit; for it is the Assembly that is the pillar and foundation of truth, and the Holy Spirit speaks through His Assembly.

"There have already arisen false prophets and false teachers who introduce destructive heresies and many will follow them. It would be better for them to have never know the truth than to have known it and turned away. People must be on their guard against these false teachers. They should obey their appointed overseers and submit to them, for they are keeping watch over their souls."

There was a long silence after which Laurentius said, "John, what you have said concerns me. I did not understand that your religion is so organized. You have said that you submit to civil authority, I know, and I do not doubt you. But I am the Roman authority on this island, and when you talk about overseers and elders and obedience; I don't know. Can I sanction correspondence within what appears to be a shadow government?"

John said nothing.

"Now it is late again," said Laurentius, "I will assign a servant to walk you back to your cave for it will soon be dark. Come back earlier tomorrow, you can come during regular hours. We can talk some more."

"That would be fine," said John.

"Well, did you talk to him about his letter?" asked Chrysippe as they prepared for bed.

"Not much," said Laurentius. "Other things seem to crop up.

"Let me ask you," he said before she could reply, "how organized are the Christians?"

"What do you mean?" she asked.

"Do they have a government?"

She thought a moment and said, "They have leaders which they call 'overseers.'"

"Is John the overseer on Patmos?" he asked.

"I suppose he must be," said Chrysippe, "though I have not heard him called so. I think an assembly must be well established in a place before it receives an overseer. I do know that different people have different functions, and, within the assembly, they are all under an overseer; so maybe John is the de facto overseer."

"What is your father's function?"

"He hosts the gatherings of the assembly," she said. "Other than that, nothing that I know; he is recently baptized, so he has no authority."

"How many attend the gatherings?" he asked. "How many Christians do I have on my island?"

"Scores," she said, "maybe hundreds, I don't really know. Why are you asking these questions?"

"Some Romans suspect the Christians of sedition," he said. "If that is the case, I cannot permit John to send his letter."

"Don't worry about that," she said. "They are like many other religions and cults in society today. They have their leaders and their peculiar ways, but they are good subjects. Some are even Roman citizens; they are not political." She extinguished the lamp, slipped into bed with him, and laid her head on his shoulder. "Be easy," she said.

# 4

# Be Forgiving, and You Will Be Forgiven

## *On the Forgiveness of Sins*

From the letters entitled Acts, Romans, 1st Corinthians 2nd Corinthians, Ephesians, Colossians, Hebrews, James, 1st Peter, 2nd Peter, 1st John, 2nd John.

*Happy the sinner whose fault is removed; whose sin is forgiven. As long as I kept silent, my bones wasted away and I groaned all day long, for your hand was heavy on me. Then I confessed my sin to you, and you removed my guilt. Would that all your faithful do the same when their hearts are heavy.*

*Psalm 32*

"Get out, all of you!" Laurentius shouted as he stormed into the marble floored office. Immediately the servants, the bureaucrats, and the petitioners shuffled out without a word. "Not you!" he said as he pointed to John. "Sit."

John waited until Laurentius plopped down on his chair and slammed his fist on the desk. Then John sat opposite the governor.

"What is wrong with my brother-in-law, John?"

"What happened?" asked the old man.

"One moment he was fine," said Laurentius, "then, for no reason, he flew into a rage. He threw things and lunged for people. He struck my wife John. My wife! Her face is bruised. For that, I will never forgive him!"

"What did you do?" asked John.

"I jumped on him from behind and clasped my arms around his. I threw him against the wall, I spun him around, and I punched him in the face. He laughed at me. At me! So, I punched him again, and again, and again. He fell to the floor and I lowered myself and kept punching him until he went limp. Then I punched him some more."

"Did you have to keep punching him?" asked John.

"I wanted to!" said Laurentius as he clinched his fists. "He struck my wife." He sat back in his chair and rubbed his hands over his face. "They pulled me off him. My father-in-law told me I should go. Once I saw that my wife was alright, I left and came here.

"John, I am a sinful man, I know this, and Apollonides is also, I have seen it, even encouraged it in past days; but Chrysippe is a good and sinless woman and her father is also sinless. How can the gods, or your God, allow this curse to fall on our family?"

"We all have sinned, governor," said John, "some more than others. But if we say we have no sin, we have deceived ourselves. We have all fallen short of the glory of God."

"Why, then, does your God allow sin?" said the governor.

"Sin entered the world through one man," said John, "the first man. And from his sin came suffering and death, even to those who sin little. But, just as through the disobedience of one man, sin entered the world, so too, through the obedience of one man, salvation entered the world."

Suppose I accept that," said Laurentius. "Suppose I accept that salvation entered the world though your Jesus. Did he not already die and pay the price for our redemption? Why, then do we still sin, and why do we still suffer?"

"Don't suppose that the Lord is slow to fulfill His promises," John said. "It is for people like you that He waits, for He is patient, and He wishes that none will parish but that all be saved by turning from their old ways. In Jesus, we have redemption through his blood, and forgiveness of our sins. You too, can turn from your old ways and your sins will be forgiven."

Laurentius smiled a wry smile. "Now you are trying to convert me, John. The other day I called you a fox; I was right." He took a deep breath.

"Look," he continued, "I don't enjoy this anger. I know anger rots a man from the inside. I have seen it. I feel it myself. I have not been so angry as I was today since Marcius betrayed me, and that anger still eats at me. I still think of Marcius and seethe. So how do I conquer my anger and my frustrations? How do I find peace?"

John looked intently at him. "Turn away from evil and turn to Jesus. He is the atonement for your sins, and not just yours, but those of the whole world."

"So, is that all there is to it; Christian magic?" asked Laurentius. "I just say 'Jesus, fix me' and I am cured? My anger will disappear? This faith that you are all so famous for, is that all I need to be saved?"

"Without faith it is impossible to please God," John said. "For whoever would draw near to him must believe that He exists and rewards those who seek Him, but faith without works is dead."

"Ah, here it comes," said Laurentius. "What works must I do to be saved; join your assembly, bow to you, donate lots of money, obey your rules?"

"Be baptized in the name of the Father, and of the Son, and of the Holy Spirit," said John, "and have your sins washed away."

"That's all? Just get wet?"

"No," said John. "Baptism is not the washing of dirt from the body, but an appeal to God for a clean conscience through the resurrection of Christ. You must be baptized, and you must turn away from your sinful ways. Do not repay evil for evil or hatred for hatred. Let all bitterness and anger and malice be drawn out of you. Be kind and tenderhearted, be forgiving and you will be forgiven. As the Lord forgives you, so you must also be forgiving. Those who are in Christ are a new creation. In them the old has passed away and the new has come. You have seen this yourself in your father-in-law."

Laurentius looked up at the ceiling, seeing nothing in particular. He looked down at his desk, seeing nothing in particular. "So," he said quietly, "if I forgive my brother-in-law for striking my wife, will I find some peace in that?"

197

"It is a start," said John.

"And if I forgive others who have harmed me, and if I return good for evil, will I have the peace my father-in-law has found?"

"You know the answer to that," said John.

There was silence for several seconds, then Laurentius spoke. "John," he said, "what is in your letter?"

"Many things," said John. "encouragements, admonishments, prophecies."

"Prophecies?" said Laurentius, "Are you speaking for God?"

"It is what he commissioned us to do," said John.

"Prophecies about what?"

"The past."

"Of the Christians?" asked Laurentius.

"Of the world. And the future."

"Of the world?"

"Of the universe. And the resurrection."

"Of Jesus?"

"Of all of us," said John.

"What do you mean?" said Laurentius. "I know you say you have seen Jesus resurrected from the dead, but that was because he was the Son of God. When we die, we are rewarded according to our deeds, but our bodies return to dirt and remain so, is that not right?"

"Just as in Adam all die" John answered, "so too, in Christ all will be raised to life, but in proper order. First Christ, who is now resurrected, then the rest of us. But first he must put all his enemies under his feet, and the last enemy is death."

Laurentius furrowed his brow. "John," he said, "Jesus was in a tomb only a short time. Others though, will have been dead and rotted away to nothing. How will they be raised? What kind of bodies will they have? Will the dirt that was once a man be reconstituted?"

"Adam's body was constituted from dirt," said John. This gave Laurentius pause. John continued, "When you sow a seed, you do not sow the plant which is to come, but a bare seed which must die before it comes to life as a plant, receiving its new body. Different bodies have different glory. There is the glory of the stars, then the moon, then the sun. So is the resurrection of the dead. It is sown as a perishable body but is raised as an imperishable body. It is sown in dishonor and weakness but is raised in glory and power. It is sown a natural body but is raised a spiritual body. Adam was from the earth, but Jesus was from the heavens. We, in birth bare the image of the earth, but in the resurrection, we will bear the image of heaven."

"How?" asked Laurentius, "When?"

John continued, "This is a mystery. It will take place in a moment, in the twinkling of eye; at the end of days, when the last trumpet sounds, and Jesus returns in glory and majesty. The dead will be raised, and we will be changed, and the prophecy will be fulfilled; 'Death is swallowed up in victory. Oh Death, where is your victory? Oh Death, where is your sting?'"

"Then what?" asked Laurentius, "What will happen after that?"

John smiled, "Eye has not seen, nor ear heard, nor has it entered into the mind of man what God has in store for those who love Him."

"And those who don't love Him?" asked Laurentius.

John lowered his eyes. "Second death."


The sun had set, and the staff had gone home, and, again, Laurentius was late at his desk. How long had he been staring out the window; an hour? He was so tired, tired of so many things.

There was a knock at the door. "Governor!"

"Come," said Laurentius.

The door opened, and two guards entered escorting a man in shackles. The man was about Laurentius' age. He was pale and gaunt, but, with some effort, he stood straight. "So, cousin," he said as their eyes met, "after two years, the time has come. No need for me to ask why you have sent for me in the night. The execution of a citizen without a trial is not something to be made public. What will it be, poison, a sword, an ax?"

"You betrayed me, Marcius," said the governor.

"Or did you betray me?" replied Marcius.

"I trusted you!" shouted the governor. He slammed his fist on the desk and Marcius flinched. "We were friends! We were family! Yet you conspired to assassinate me. And for what? For control of this little rock of an island? For my half of our uncle's small inheritance? What made it worth it to you?"

"We have gone over this," said Marcius. "It doesn't matter now, since I will be dead soon."

"Maybe I should have tried you two years ago," said the governor. "You would have been executed back then.'

"Or exonerated," said Marcius. "I have a right to trial! Why did you not give me my trial?"

"Because of your mother, my aunt!" said Laurentius. "And because of your wife, and your daughter. I did not want your shame on them."

"But poverty you don't mind," said Marcius. "I have gotten some small news over the two years since I have seen them. They have nothing left without me to support them. They linger in Ephesus as servants of a distance relative. My daughter was eighteen and betrothed. But it was broken off when her dowry went to my creditors. Now she has no future, thanks to you."

"Well tonight it ends," said the governor.

"I am ready," said the prisoner.

"Release him," said Laurentius.

"What is this?" asked Marcius as the guards removed his shackles.

Laurentius held up a small packet of papers without looking at Marcius. "Here," he said. "This is a full pardon for you, your citizenship paper, passage to Ephesus, and some other papers you will need on your journey. Go get your family and then sail to Sicily. There will be an office job for you at an olive oil factory."

Marcius was stunned, He slowly took the papers. "Why?' he said.

"And here," said Laurentius has he tossed a pouch on the desk. "It is enough to get you all to Sicily and to provide a modest dowry for your daughter."

"Why?" repeated Marcius.

"Your ship leaves on the morning tide," said Laurentius, "be on it. Never come back. Never attempt to communicate. Never get into politics. Now, go."

"But why?" asked Marcius.

Laurentius shook his head, "God only knows."

# 5

# Faith, Hope, and Love

## *On the Christian Life*

From the letters entitled 1st Corinthians, 2nd Corinthians, Galatians, Philippians, Colossians, and 1st Timothy.

*How precious is your love, oh God! We take refuge in the shadow of your wings. We feast on the bounty of your house; from your crystal streams you give us drink. For with you is the fountain of life and in your light, we see light. Maintain your kindness towards your friends and your just defense of the honest hearted.*

*Psalm 36*

The atrium of the house of Laurentius was the finest on the island with Ionic columns, a bubbling fountain, and fragrant shrubs whose scents mingled in the still air of dusk.

"It was a lovely meal governor," said John as the servants disappeared into the house carrying plates and bowls. "Thank you for inviting me."

"It was a debt paid to my wife," said Laurentius, "But," he stuttered "I am happy to have your company."

"You seem happy," said John, "Has something happened?"

"I was relieved of a burden," said Laurentius.

"Then you have forgiven Apollonides?"

"That too," said Laurentius as he placed his goblet on the table next to him. He was alone with John; men talking among men as was customary, but he knew Chrysippe was nearby; most likely lurking and watching and listening as best she could.

"John," said Laurentius, "are you going to baptize my wife as you did her father?"

"If she asks."

"Have you baptized her brother?"

"No," said John. "Apollonides is no longer friendly to me. He avoids me."

"I think it is likely," said Laurentius, "that Chrysippe may ask to be baptized." He waited for a reply but received none. "Tell me then," he continued, "what is required of Christians from their overseers."

"Faith in Christ," said John, "and love."

"Love of what?"

"Love of all," answered John.

"No," said Laurentius, "I mean, what kind of love. You know some accuse you Christians of incest. Because you call your wives 'sisters' they think you are marrying your sisters. I know better than that, but I do not really know what you mean by 'love.' There are so many kinds; brotherly love, love of country, love of pleasure, sexual love. What is Christian love?"

"Yes," said John, "there are those types of common love but, I will tell you of a more excellent way. If I speak with the voice of an angel but do not have love, I am a noisy gong or clashing symbol. If I have the gift of prophesy and if I know all things, if I have faith enough to move mountains, but do not have love, I have nothing. If I give away all that I have, but do not have love, I gain nothing.

"Love is patient, love is kind, it is not jealous, it is not arrogant, it does not seek its own gain, it is not provoked, it does not brood over injuries, it does not rejoice over wrong doing, but rejoices in the truth; it bears all things, believes all things, endures all things. Love never fails.

"Prophecies will end. Languages will cease. Knowledge will fade. In the end, three things remain; faith, hope, and love, and the greatest of these is love."

Laurentius paused, "You bother me, John. First you tell me that one must have faith that there is One God and, in the form of a man, he died to save us from our own sins; then you tell me that such faith, without good works, is dead; then you tell me that those good works, without love, are nothing. I would say that you and yours are all crazy fools; but I must admit, the change I have seen in my father-in-law is profound, even miraculous." He glanced around the atrium. "I am also starting to see a change in my wife. She is less anxious these days.

"So, John," he said, "there is a change of faith and a change of attitude. What else changes? Are there rules? Rituals? What will be expected of my wife?"

"We gather regularly, as you know," John said.

"And at these gatherings, you eat a meal?" asked Laurentius.

"We have our own houses in which to eat and drink regular meals," said John. "When we gather, we gather to eat the Lord's supper."

"What makes that different?" asked Laurentius. "Some accuse you of cannibalism. I do not believe it, but you must explain to me what happens."

"We drink from the cup of blessing which is a participation in the blood of Christ, and we eat the bread which is a participation in the body of Christ," said John.

"You can see," said Laurentius, "how some can call that cannibalism."

John shook his head. "On the night in which Jesus was betrayed, at the Passover supper, which commemorates the night in which the Israelites ate the flesh of the sacrificed lamb whose blood saved them, he took the bread and broke it and gave thanks and said 'Take this and eat it, this is my body, which is for you; do this in remembrance of me'. Then he took the cup, saying 'This cup is the new covenant in my blood; do this in remembrance of me.' You see, Jesus is our Passover lamb that was sacrificed, so as often as we eat the bread and drink the cup, we proclaim the death of the Lord until he returns."

"Has my wife partaken in that way?"

"No," said John. "She has not been sanctified in baptism. Whoever eats or drinks the cup of the Lord in an unworthy manner, shall be guilty of the body and blood of Jesus. Some who do, become sick, or even die. Someday she may be worthy."

"Those among you who partake unworthily, can they be made worthy?" asked Laurentius.

"Through Christ, God reconciled the world to Himself, not holding their sins against them," said John. "We have been given the ministry of reconciliation and we are ambassadors of God. Therefore, we confess our sins to each other and if anyone has sinned, a priest prays over him and his sins are forgiven. And if anyone is sick, the priest anoints him with oil and prays over him, for the prayers of a righteous man accomplish much."

"How is one made a priest in your religion?" asked Laurentius.

John answered, "Overseers, or bishops, and elders, or priests, and servers, or deacons are appointed and receive their authority when existing overseers or elders place their hands on them and pray over them."

"John," said Laurentius, "if Chrysippe is baptized and becomes a Christian, how will that affect our marriage?"

"She will remain your wife and her devotion to you will increase. And, if someday, you are baptized, your devotion to her will increase; for marriage is held in high honor among us. Wives are to be subordinate to their husbands in all things. Just as the Assembly is subordinate to Christ, so the wife should be subordinate to her husband. Husbands are to love their wives just as Christ loves the Assembly. He is to keep her pure and blameless. Husbands are to love their wives as they love their own bodies; nourishing and cherishing them, just as Christ does the Assembly. A man who loves his wife, loves himself. So, a man should love his wife as himself and a wife should honor her husband."

"Well, that at least is comforting," said Laurentius. How else, is a Christian to live? Be specific so I can know."

"We are to be doers of the word of God, not just hearers of the word," said John. "We are to abandon what is earthly in us; sexual immorality, impurity, passion, evil desire, and covetousness, anger, wrath, malice, slander, extra marital sex, homosexuality, thievery, drunkenness, effeminate behavior, and lying, for these are not things of love; but, things of passion and desire. The desires of the body are against the spirit of the soul and those who persist in such things will not inherit the kingdom of God, for just as the body rots, so too, those who follow such things. But just as the spirit lives forever, so too, those who follow the spirit. And the fruits of the spirit are love, joy, peace, patience, kindness, goodness, faithfulness, gentleness, self-control, compassionate hearts, humility, meekness.

"Whatever is true, whatever is honorable, whatever is just, whatever is pure, whatever is lovely, whatever is commendable, if there is any excellence, if there is anything worthy of praise, we strive to practice these things, and the God of peace is always with us."

Chrysippe came out from the house followed by a servant girl. They were both wrapped in cloaks. "The children are in bed," she said as she placed a hand on her husband's shoulder, "They're waiting for you to say good night. I'm going to my father's. I'm worried about Apollonides."

"I can come with you," said Laurentius.

"No," she said as she glanced at John, "You two have things to discuss. It will be alright." She said goodbye to John, and they watched her leave.

"That woman manipulates me you know," said Laurentius.

John shrugged.

Laurentius smiled. "I'll see to the children. I'll be back soon."

# 6

# Give All Your Cares to Him, For He Cares For You

## On Prayer

From the letters entitled Romans, 2nd Thessalonians, Hebrews, James, and 1st Peter.

*Blessed be the Lord who has heard the sound of my pleading. The Lord is my strength and my shield. In Him I trusted and have found help. My heart rejoices. I praise my God in song.*

*Psalm 28*

"It is a blessing," said John, when Laurentius returned, "that, under your governorship, two women, such as your wife and servant, can walk the streets of the town after sunset."

"I would be a failure if that were not possible," said Laurentius as he sat.

"You know," he said with a mild smile, "every night before bed, she raises her hands and prays for me, that I be a good man, and a good governor. I don't know if your God hears her, but it comforts me nonetheless."

"Do you pray?" asked John.

"Why?" said Laurentius. "The gods of Rome don't hear me; so, there is no reason to pray to them. The god of the Christians already knows everything; so, there is no reason to pray to him."

"You have never prayed?" asked John.

"Never," said Laurentius. Even during the rites of our religion, it is the priest or priestess or oracle that prays, not me. I have never prayed."

"How lonely you must be," said John.

"I have never been lonely," said Laurentius, "I have a family, friends, and now I have a family of my own. I am the governor; wherever I go on this island, I am never alone."

"But you are alone in the universe," replied John. "Since my earliest recollections, I understood that God is in all, and through all, so I have never been alone, even when no man is near. As Christians, we know this, that God is always with us, so we pray constantly."

"We are talking now," said Laurentius, "so you cannot be praying."

"If I followed you wherever you went," said John, would you not always feel my presence even though you were not directly talking to me? There are many ways to pray; in our minds, with our lips, in our actions; and God hears all."

"Very well then," said Laurentius after a pause, "I will concede that, if God is always present, then a Christian can always be praying, even if just in the back of his mind; but, why bother? If God knows everything, he already knows what you will pray for and he already knows if he will grant it. So why bother asking?"

"You are a father," John said, "God is father. Think like a father and answer your own question."

Laurentius shook his head and said, "John you are a fox. I used to think I was the hunter to your fox, but maybe I am the prey." He took a sip of wine and a deep breath. "Very well. I have taught my children to be gracious, so they ask instead of demand. I have taught them to be respectful, so sometimes I require they ask for things they want, even though I already know that I will give it. I have taught them to be grateful, so they always say, "thank you," and not just to me or their mother."

"Good," said John. "And at the end of the day, you ask them how their days went even though you can be fairly sure of the answer. You do this, not because you want to hear a report of their mundane and childish routines; but because you want to hear their voices as they talk to you; because you simply love to have their attention and you love when they share with you. Therefore, we pray in many ways and for many reasons."

"Don't ask me to pray John," said Laurentius, "That is too personal. Besides, I would feel a fool if there is no Christian God and I was talking to nobody. Anyway, I have so many cares, I would not know where to begin."

"John smiled, "Give Him all your cares, for he cares for you. The Spirit helps us in our doubt. We often do not know what to pray for as we should, but the Spirit Himself intercedes for us with emotions too deep for words."

"I am a sinful man, John. He will not listen to me."

John answered, "All have sinned. If we confess our sins, he is faithful and just, and forgives our sins, and cleanses them from us. And if we learn His will, and ask anything from Him, according to His will, He hears us. If you lack the knowledge of the will of God, ask God, who gives generously, and it will be given to you. Then you can approach God's throne with grace and confidence and receive mercy and help in your needs. Then you can rejoice always, praying constantly, giving thanks, being watchful in prayer, making petitions, interceding for all people, and the peace of God which surpasses all understanding will guard your heart and your mind in Jesus Christ."

"I knew it," said Laurentius, "I knew you want to make me a Christian."

"Don't be silly," said John, "I want all people to know the peace of Christ, this is obvious. You are no exception. But for now, I just want you to allow me to send out my letter."

"You must appreciate my position," said Laurentius, happy to change the subject, even to this. "You may be free to come and go on this island, but I am your jailer. You have been sent to my keeping because you have spread Christianity and the emperor hates Christians. I am ultimately responsible to that same emperor, the one who hates Christians. My job is to keep you out of the way. What do you think would happen to me and my family if word got out that I was complicit in the spreading of a doctrine that the Emperor finds subversive? John, I like you. You have done nothing but good since you have been here, and I have learned much from you. Our talks have been good for me and your presence has been good for my family. But all that can be undone if I were to lose my position, or worse.

"John, I have an idea. The emperor is an old man; he will not live much longer and none of his likely successors appear to hate your religion. When the Emperor dies, you will be pardoned, and you can go and deliver your letter in person."

"I am an old man," said John.

"I thought of that," said Laurentius. "On this you must trust me; find a place of safe keeping on this island for your letter. Tell me where that will be and, if you should die before the Emperor, I give you my word that, when he dies, I will see your is letter delivered."

At that moment, a man burst into the atrium. Laurentius recognized him as a friend of his father-in-law. He was red faced and panting. "John,' he said, "something terrible has happened."

"What has happened?" said Laurentius.

The man turned to him as if he had just seen him. "In your father-in-law's house," he said, "Apollonides has gone completely mad. Several of us were enjoying the evening in his atrium. Everything was fine. Then, some-one mentioned Jesus Christ and Apollonides screamed and covered his ears as if a loud trumpet had blasted in his face. He began to rant; shouting curses and blasphemies, saying 'That man is a pig and his mother was a whore.' He pushed over the table that held the refreshments and picked it up and threw it at his father. He leapt onto an old man striking him on the head. He called us piglets and fools and he said the demons will feast on us and our children. Then he ran into the house toward the women and children who were there."

Laurentius sprang to his feet, but John held his arm.

"Were they harmed?" asked John.

"No," said the man. "We fell on him; six of us. He was so strong! We held him down and he struggled. He never stopped shouting. Blood oozed from his eyes like tears. We began to tire, but he appeared to grow even stronger. Someone brought a cord and we bound him, but in a moment, he broke the cords! We bound him three times and three times he broke his bindings. More men, hearing the commotion, came in from the street and they relieved us. Someone said to find John and I came because I had heard you would be here. There were eight heavy men sitting on him when I left, but he showed no sign of tiring."

"Let us go!" said the governor.

"Wait Laurentius!" John said. "Please, stay here, I will go."

"How could you ask such a thing?" said Laurentius.

"Listen, my friend," said the Apostle, "You are a man of strength and of action. But your kind of strength cannot help Apollonides. In fact, it will only be an obstacle. You stay, and I will go, and it will be well. On this you must trust me."

"But then," said Laurentius, "what am I to do?"

John laid a firm hand on his shoulder and said, "Pray."

# 7

# I Make All Things New

## *The Letter*

### From the Letter Entitled Revelation

*The Lord's throne is established in Heaven. God's power rules over all. Bless the Lord all you angels; powerful and obedient! Bless the Lord, you multitudes; all who do God's will! Bless the Lord all you creatures; you who dwell in God's domain! Bless the Lord, oh my soul!*

*Psalm 103*

The tiny ray of sunlight that had earlier peeked into the cave was now a flood of daylight that filled the space, showing it to be tidy and comfortable, if not actually clean. The object which had appeared black and blurry in the grainy pre-dawn gray was shown to be a length of a wool blanket that slowly raised and lowered in a barely perceptible rhythm. Out from under one end poked a bare foot. Out from under the other end laid a ball of gray hair, long in the Jewish fashion.

Laurentius had not slept. The air was chilly, and his feet were wet from dewy grass; yet, he was content. For some reason he was not sleepy, so he sat patiently and waited.

The rhythm of the blanket suddenly stopped and the bare foot twitched. The gray ball moved a bit and an arm appeared from under the blanket. There was more motion and the torso of John, the old Apostle, arose, pushed up by one arm. He glanced around and spotted Laurentius. He blinked and stared a moment.

"You did it," said Laurentius.

"You look terrible," said John.

Laurentius looked down at himself. His sandals were muddy as was the lower edge of his wrinkled cloak. His hands were black with charcoal and he could just barely see the tip of his nose which was also black. He supposed much of his face and clothes were similarly blackened and he knew he was unshaved, and his hair must be unkempt. "But, you did it," he said.

John raised his head and sniffed. "Something smells good."

"Oh," said Laurentius, "I have been keeping some mulled wine and porridge warm for you. You know, it's not easy to light a fire and cook a meal in silence and darkness; but I did it."

"Don't be so proud," said John. "Any woman could have done a better job. But," he said as he perked up, "I thank you." He rose and went straight to the fire to examine the meal. He picked up two bowls. "Would you like some?"

"Yes please."

John ladled out some porridge and some wine and handed it to Laurentius.

"You did it," said Laurentius.

John rolled his eyes. "That is the third time you said that. What do you suppose that I did?"

"Chrysippe came home to me just a few minutes after you left last night," said Laurentius. "I have never seen her in such distress. Her face was dripping with tears as she fell into my arms. She was hysterical and incoherent for some time, so I held her and waited. She kept calling her brother's name, as if he were just out in the street. My heart was breaking for her, but I am a man and a husband, so I held fast. After some time, I had wine brought to her and tried to find out what was going on, but she could add nothing to what I already knew; except that you told her to go home. A half hour or so had passed before time, and the wine, calmed her heart a little. We were still in the atrium. She knelt and pulled me down beside her, and she began to pray. She prayed to your god for her only living brother; the baby she rocked; the boy she chased; the youth she comforted when their grandmother died; the man who comforted her when their sister died. She bared her soul and poured out emotion like a flood. I have never seen … never seen."

"Did you pray?" asked John.

"I felt her sorrow because I shared it," said Laurentius. "He comforted her when their sister died, but who do you think comforted him? Who advised him when he first fell in love? Who sent him to university? Who got him his first real job? Who gave him attention back in the days when his father was too busy?"

"Did you pray?" asked John.

"I was feeling helpless," said Laurentius, "a feeling that is strange to me; that I hate.

"About two hours, maybe three, after you left, someone came running to our house. I was prepared for the worst; but he was elated. He said that Apollonides was healed and well. He said my father-in-law had sent for us. We went as fast as we could to the house and we found Apollonides, sitting at table eating and drinking, surrounded by friends and neighbors. Some were drinking and laughing with him and my father-in-law. Others just sat, as if they were confused. The place was a shamble from the struggle, but no one cared at that time.

"I saw him, John. I saw his face. His eyes were clear, and his wit was sharp. It was like the time when he won a race and a laurel crown; he was exhausted but elated. The anger and hate that had covered his eyes were gone and he embraced me like a brother.

"After we had been convinced that we were not dreaming, the story was related to us: after his first attack, Apollonides had calmed down and started to joke. They thought his spell had passed and were about to let him up, but then you walked in and his fury returned with a greater strength. He shouted more curses and foul condemnations and he slammed his head again and again onto the tile floor as if he was trying to kill himself. You plopped on him hard enough to break his ribs, but he did not notice. You grabbed him by the hair and shouted into his face 'what is your name?'

He screamed and spat on you and blew snot on you and you slapped his face and repeated 'What is your name?' He screamed 'Apollonides!' You slapped him again and shouted into his face 'In the name of Jesus of Nazareth, what is your name?'

"The accounts became confused at this time. Though the witnesses were all present, their testimony differed. Some said they heard him shout an unpronounceable name in a voice that was not his own. Others said they heard gurgling from his throat. Others said he roared like a beast. But then their accounts agreed again. You said, 'Get out and go away,' and Apollonides shrieked and vomited huge amounts of blood. Then he fainted for a few seconds and, when he regained his wits, he looked as if he did not know where he was or what had happened. He was his old self again. People came with jugs of water and clean clothes and, all the time they were cleaning him up, my brother-in-law was thanking you and praising God. They said you left just a few minutes before we arrived.

"He is back, John. My brother-in-law, my brother, we have him back, he is free, and you did it."

"If a growth is removed from the skin," said John, "who did it; the scalpel or the doctor?"

"The doctor, of course," said Laurentius, 'a scalpel can do nothing on its own."

"So, who brought your brother back, me or God?"

Laurentius smiled slightly. "John," he said, "let me read your letter."

"I cannot," said John, "it is not for you."

"Then tell me what is in it."

"I cannot," said John, "I will not abridge the word of God."

Laurentius' shoulder dropped.

"But I can do this," said the Apostle. "My letter is a telling of a vision I had that I was commanded to write down. I cannot share with you what is written; that is for believers. But I can share with you some of what I saw, not from the letter, but from my imperfect memory. Perhaps it will be a down payment against the time when you will be able to read it in its entirety, with your own eyes."

"I am listening," said Laurentius.

John took a deep breath and placed a finger on his cheek. "I saw an open door to Heaven," he said, "and I heard a voice like a trumpet. It said, 'come up, and I will show you what will take place.' Instantly I was in spirit. I saw a throne, and the One on the throne was like a gem, and a rainbow encircled the throne. Lightning and thunder came from the throne and around it was a sea of crystal. Beside the throne were four creatures of great power; the first was like a lion, the second was like a bull, the third was like a man, and the fourth was like an eagle. And around the throne were twenty-four smaller thrones, and on each throne was an elder clothed in white with a gold crown on his head. And the four creatures would sing praises to the One on the throne, who lives forever, and the twenty-four elders would cast their crowns down and worship the One on the throne.

"And in the hand of the One on the throne was a book sealed with seven seals, and a mighty angel loudly said, 'Who is worthy to break the seals of the book and open it?' And there was none in Heaven or on Earth worthy to touch it. Then I saw, as from the throne, a lamb, standing as if slain. He took the book, and as he did, the four creatures and the twenty-four elders bowed down before the lamb with harps and songs. They burned incense to the lamb and the smoke was the prayers of the people of God. And they said, 'You are worthy to open the book, for with your blood you purchased the souls of people from around the world for God.' And uncounted angels were there saying, 'Worthy is the Lamb who was slain!' and every creature in Heaven and on Earth, and under the Earth, and in the sea, and all creatures worshipped He who is on the throne and the Lamb.

"The Lamb broke the first seal of the book and a rider on a white horse appeared with a bow in his hand. He went out in power to conquer.

"The Lamb broke the second seal and a rider on a red horse appeared with a sword in his hand. He went all around the Earth causing war and men killed each other.

"The Lamb broke the third seal and a rider on a black horse appeared with a pair of scales in his hand. He caused famine and poverty.

"The Lamb broke the fourth seal and a rider on an ashen horse appeared and his name was Death. He went out and killed a fourth of mankind.

"Then the Lamb broke the fifth seal and I saw below the throne the souls of those who had been killed because of the Word of God. And they said, 'How long, Lord, before you avenge our blood on those who live on the Earth?' And they were given white robes and told to rest easy until the number of them is fulfilled.

"Then the Lamb broke the sixth seal and there was a great earthquake; and the sun darkened, and the moon turned red, and stars fell from the sky, and the sky split apart. And men hid in caves and said to the caves, 'Fall on us and hide us from God and the Lamb, for the judgement day has come.'

"Then I saw a great multitude, too many to count, from every nation and language on Earth; clothed in white and waving palm branches and praising He who is on the throne and the Lamb. And their praises were joined by all the angels, the elders, and the four creatures.

"And one of the elders said to me, 'who are these clothed in white?' and I said, 'Lord, I do not know, but you know.' He said, 'These are those who have endured the tribulation, and they have washed their robes and made them white in the blood of the Lamb. They shall hunger and thirst no more, nor shall the sun beat upon them, for the Lamb shall be their shepherd and shall lead them to life giving waters and shall wipe every tear from their eyes.'

"Then the Lamb broke the seventh seal and there was silence in Heaven for a half hour. And an altar was before the throne and an angel came before the alter and took the incense burner and he added incense to the prayers of the people of God and the smoke of the prayers of the angel and the people of God went up before God on the throne. And the angel filled the incense burner with fire and threw it down to Earth causing thunder and lightning and an earthquake.

"And there were seven angels with seven trumpets. The first trumpet sounded and there appeared hail and fire mixed with blood and it was hurled to the Earth and a third of the Earth, and a third of the people, were burnt up.

"The second trumpet sounded, and a fiery mountain was thrown into the sea and the sea became like blood.

"The third trumpet sounded, and a star fell to Earth in burning flame. And it fell on a third of the fresh water and made it bitter and many died from the water because it became poison.

"The fourth trumpet sounded and a third of the sun and the moon and the stars were darkened, and the days and nights were darkened as well.

"The fifth trumpet sounded and on Earth a bottomless pit was opened, and smoke came out of it and darkened the sky. And out from the pit came stinging locusts to torment men, and the men longed to die but could not.

"The sixth trumpet sounded, and four angels were released and in war and fire, killed a third of mankind, but those who were left did not change from their evil ways and they continued to oppose God.

"The seventh trumpet sounded, and I heard loud voices saying, 'The kingdom of the world has become the kingdom of the Lord and His Messiah, and He will reign forever!' And the twenty-four elders said, 'Thank you Almighty One that, in your great power, you have begun to reign.'

"The temple of God in Heaven was open and in it, in lightning and thunder, appeared the Ark of His new covenant; a woman, clothed with the sun and with the moon under her feet, and on her head a crown of twelve stars; and she was about to give birth. A great red dragon appeared, and its tail swept away a third of the stars; and it waited for the woman to give birth, so it could devour the child. She gave birth to a son who is to rule all the nations. The child was taken up to Heaven and the woman was protected from the dragon and made safe.

"Michael and his angels waged war against the dragon and his demons and the dragon, who is Satan who deceives the whole world, and his demons, were thrown down to the Earth for there was no longer a place for them in Heaven. And the dragon was furious at the woman, and went off to wage war against her children who are those who hold to the word of Jesus. And a beast came out of the sea to serve the dragon and oppose the people of God. And the dragon gave the beast his authority and people saw his power and worshipped him. And he made war against the people of God and overcame them and was worshipped throughout the Earth except for those who were the people of God. And a second beast came from the earth to replace the first, and it exercised all the authority of the first beast and made signs and wonders, even calling fire from the sky, so to deceive those living on Earth.

"The dragon and the beast gathered the armies of the world to do battle against the army of God and they gathered at a valley that in Hebrew is called Armageddon. A loud voice came out of the temple in Heaven from the throne saying, 'It is finished!" And there were flashes of lightning and peals of thunder and the Earth shook as has never been done before. The cities of the nations fell, and every island disappeared, and every mountain was gone, and hundred-pound hail stones fell to the Earth. And I saw Heaven open and out came a rider on a white horse and he is called Faithful and True, and he judges and wages war. His eyes were of flame and on his head were many jeweled crowns and he wore clothes dipped in blood and his name was The Word of God. He was followed by the armies of heaven dressed in clean white linen and riding white horses. From his mouth came a sword of truth to strike the nations and their leaders, so to rule all nations.

"The beast and the leaders and the armies of the Earth were assembled to meet them. The beast was taken and cast into a lake of fire and all the rest were killed by the sword which comes from the mouth of Him who sat on the white horse; and crows came and ate their bodies.

"And I saw an angel come down from Heaven with mighty chains. He seized the dragon, the serpent of old, and bound him for a thousand years. Then I saw the souls of those who had been executed for not worshipping the beast. They were resurrected and reigned with Christ for a thousand years and will be the priests of God.

"When the thousand years were complete, Satan was released to deceive the nations of the Earth once more. And he gathered them again to make war against the holy ones, and their numbers were like the sands of the beach. They surrounded the camp of the people of God, but fire came down from Heaven and destroyed them. Then Satan was thrown into the lake of fire with the beast and they will remain there in torment for ever and ever.

"I saw the throne of God. And the sea gave up its dead and the earth gave up its dead; great and small. All were standing before the throne of God as books were opened, and they all were judged according to their deeds as written in the books. And Death and Hell were thrown into the lake of fire along with all those whose names were not written in the Book of Life.

"Then I saw a new Heaven and a new Earth, for the old Heaven and Earth had passed away. And I saw the Holy City, a New Jerusalem, come down from God adorned like a bride. I heard a loud voice say, 'God shall dwell among men and they will be his people. He will wipe away every tear and there shall be no more death, nor mourning, nor crying, nor pain, for the old things have passed away.' Then, the One on the throne said, 'I make all things new. I am the beginning and the end.' And I was taken to a high mountain and saw the New Jerusalem. It shown with the glory of God and looked like a brilliant gem. It was made of precious stones and gems and the streets were of pure gold. There was no temple in the city, for God and the Lamb are its temple. There was no need for the sun or moon to shine their lights; for God was the light of the city. Nothing unclean was in the city nor any sin. A river of the water of life, clear as crystal, came from the throne of God and the Lamb and flowed through the center of the city. On either side of the river were trees that always gave fruit.

"The throne of God and the Lamb shall be in the city and the people will see His face. And there shall be no night and no need of lamps; for God shall be the light of the people and they will reign with Him forever.

"And I heard Jesus say, 'I am coming quickly. My reward is with me to give to every man according to his deeds. I am the first and the last, the beginning and the end. Blessed are those who wash their robes and have the right to enter into the city.' And I heard the Spirit say, 'Come, let whoever wishes take the water of life without cost.'"

There was silence for a long moment. John blinked and looked about as if he had just awakened from a dream. Then he focused on his listener. "So, my friend," he said, "you have heard the Good News of Jesus Christ. The Holy Spirit has laid this gift of truth before you to do with as you see fit. Have you been moved? Or have you been wasting your time? You have a decision to make. What do you say?"

If you have found this Inquirer's Bible helpful, please help us out by going to your point of purchase and writing a review. It would be a quick and easy way for you to help bring this book to the attention of a person who is looking for something just like it.

Made in the USA
Monee, IL
10 November 2020